THE FORMATION OF

THE ORANGE ORDER

1795 - 1798

GOLI Publications

THE FORMATION OF

THE ORANGE ORDER

1795 - 1798

The edited papers of Colonel William Blacker
and Colonel Robert H. Wallace

Published by
the Education Committee of
The Grand Orange Lodge of Ireland

GOLI Publications
The Grand Orange Lodge of Ireland
65 Dublin Road, Belfast. BT2 7HE

© The Grand Orange Lodge of Ireland 1994

First Published 1994
Reprinted 1999

**British Library Cataloguing-in-Publication Data.
A catalogue record for this book is
available from the British Library.**

Blacker, William & Wallace, Robert Hugh
    The Formation of the Orange Order 1795-1798
    1. Orangeism - Ireland - History
    I. Title
    941'.5'07

ISBN 0 9501444 3 6

CONTENTS

ACKNOWLEDGEMENTS

The Blacker Day Books:

Publication of the extracts from the Blacker Day book by kind permission of the Armagh County Museum.

The Wallace Papers:

Publication of the Wallace Papers by kind permission of The Wallace Estate and the Deputy Keeper of the Records, Public Record Office of Northern Ireland.

ooOoo

The Education Committee of the Grand Orange Lodge of Ireland acknowledges with thanks the assistance given by the Armagh County Museum and the Public Record Office of Northern Ireland, in providing access to the original documents and permitting publication. Appreciation is expressed to Catherine McCullough, Curator of the Armagh County Museum, for her careful proof reading of the extracts of the Blacker Day Books. The Family of the late Colonel Wallace, and particularly his youngest daughter Mrs Jean Acworth, are thanked for giving permission for publication and for their encouragement and support.

The Research Group of the Grand Royal Arch Purple Chapter of Ireland are thanked for their role in initiating the whole project and conducting the initial negotiations with the Public Record Office and Mrs Jean Acworth. Thanks also to Ballymacash LOL 317 for the use of the portrait of Bro. Rev. Philip Johnston, Lisburn Cathedral for the use of the silhouette of Bro. Rev. Snowden Cupples and Mr. M. H. St.C. Harnett for the use of the portrait of Bro. Rev. Dean Waring. Bro. David Cargo and his daughter Mrs Elizabeth Jackson are thanked for proof reading and typing the Wallace Papers from photostat copies of the original manuscripts.

Cecil Kilpatrick
(Editor)
Rev. Brian Kennaway
(Convenor - Education Committee)

PREFACE

These papers are published as a contribution to the celebration of the bicentenary of the Battle of the Diamond and the birth of the Orange Order in 1795.

The Wallace papers are particularly valuable for a number of reasons.

Firstly, unlike the present generation, he was able to visit the area where these events had occurred and speak to old men, who in their youth had heard the first hand accounts of the men who had fought the battle and founded the Order.

Secondly, he recorded the views not only of the later leaders who were mostly educated men of the landed gentry, but also of the farmers, weavers and linen merchants who made up the initial membership.

Thirdly, unlike other historians who record several conflicting accounts of these events, he comes down with a definite conclusion after weighing up the evidence.

The tragedy is that he never completed his work and that the first part has been lost. For that reason, in an attempt to partially fill the void, Colonel Blacker's account of the Battle of the Diamond has been included as a curtain raiser. He sets the scene for Colonel Wallace's manuscript which picks up immediately after the battle.

BIOGRAPHICAL NOTE ON

COLONEL WILLIAM BLACKER
1777 - 1855

William Blacker was the first member of the gentry to join the Order. When only 18 he carried ammunition to the battlefield at the Diamond and was then initiated. The Colonel's answers at the 1835 Enquiry make interesting reading:

> 8928. Are you a member of the Orange society? - I am.
> 8929. How long have you been so? - It wants about six weeks of 40 years.

> 8940. Were you on the spot when the Battle was fought? - I was not in time to be under fire, but immediately as it was terminating.

> 8943. What did you see at the Diamond? - When I got up I saw the Defenders making off in one direction and the firing had nearly ceased, I may say had ceased except a dropping shot or two, and I saw a number of dead bodies.
> 8944. Can you state the number? - No; they were conveying them away upon cars in different directions, so that I could not make an exact calculation.
> 8945. Where there 50? - No; if there were 30 killed, that was the outside.

> 8955. How long did the engagement last? - I do not think the actual engagement lasted about 15 minutes perhaps.
> 8956. Was the first Orange Lodge formed then? - It was.
> 8957. Where? - I understood it was formed in the house of a man named Sloan, in the village of Loughgall.(*)

(*) "Report of the Select Committee of the House of Commons appointed to enquire into the Nature, Character, Extent and Tendency of Orange Lodges, Associations or Societies in Ireland, Great Britain, and the Colonies" 1835. [Page 213 - 214 1st August 1835]

He obtained "No. 12" for a Lodge at Carrickblacker and two years later became the first County Grand Master of Armagh.

While still a student at Trinity College, Dublin, he was entrusted by the Government with arms to equip a Company of Orangemen who became the Seagoe Yeomanry. As a Captain he led them into action against the insurgents at Naas in Co. Kildare. He then recruited and helped raise the Armagh Regiment of Militia becoming its Colonel. All this time he remained County Grand Master of Armagh, a position he valued higher than any other in the Institution.

In 1832, with the passing of the Great Reform Bill, a hostile Government passed an Act to prohibit "Party Processions". When the Portadown Orangemen decided to demonstrate in Carrickblacker demesne, he did his duty as a magistrate by ordering them to disperse. Although he wore no Orange insignia, his wife and the ladies of his household stood behind him wearing orange lilies. For this crime he was dismissed from the Commission of the Peace on the advice of Lord Gosford the anti Orange Governor of the County.

He was of a poetic bent and regarded as the bard of the Order. His works include "The Diamond will be Trumps Again" beginning "There was a time when 'twas no crime." He also wrote "No Surrender" beginning "Behold the crimson banner floats" and "Oliver's Advice".

The family's Orange tradition was carried on by the Colonel's heir and nephew Bro. Stewart Blacker, who was Grand Secretary of the Grand Orange Lodge, and who also gave evidence to the House of Commons Enquiry in 1835. Colonel Wallace gives further information on the Colonel's life under the heading "First Grand Master", reproduced on pages 103 and 104.

Lt. Colonel William Blacker
From *The Dublin University Magazine,xvii* (January to June, 1841)

INTRODUCTION TO
THE BLACKER DAY BOOKS

In the Armagh County Museum are preserved seven large leather bound volumes which Colonel Blacker called his Day Books. These are filled with his hand written accounts of his thoughts, when he reflected on past events, and records of his day to day activities. He records copies of his correspondence and drafts of the sermons he preached. The writing is far from being copper plate but it is legible with care and patience. The reader is rewarded by feeling that he is in touch with the original handwriting of the author and better able to understand him. His account of the Battle of the Diamond is contained in the first volume, in Chapters ten and eleven, commencing on page 220 and finishing on page 240.

It can be dated by the fact that it is followed by a copy of a letter he wrote to Lady Roden at Tollymore Park which is dated 30th November, 1836. She was the wife of the famous Third Earl of Roden who was involved in the monster rally at Hillsborough in 1834 and Dolly's Brae in 1849.

One of the greatest differences between Colonel Blacker's account and that written half a century later by Colonel Wallace, is in the part played by James Wilson of the Dyan. All the accounts written by the gentlemen of the time play down the role of the Orange Boys. It must be remembered that the French Revolution of 1789 had filled them with a fear of all popular, peasant led movements. They wrongly assumed that James Wilson and the Orange Boys were Peep of Day Boys, who were responsible for disturbances and the wrecking of houses and looms. After his account of the battle Colonel Blacker goes on to relate in considerable detail some of these outrages, which he deplores in no uncertain terms.

In Blacker's view the New Order was a completely new departure, unconnected with the Orange Boys or any other body. Colonel Wallace's more mature reflection written for a later generation, gives a more balanced view. He gives credit where it is due, to the men of the Dyan and the Diamond, who had borne the burden and heat of the day, before the gentlemen took over the leadership and gave it direction and purpose.

THE BATTLE OF THE DIAMOND

by

COLONEL WILLIAM BLACKER.

Before I proceed with immediate details of the Battle of the Diamond, it may be right to give some particulars of the country for a short time before it. The first time that the Romanists showed any signs of making head after the enactment of the Penal Laws was in the year 1759, when the White Boys' Association commenced its career. Its first demonstrations were made so exactly with the sailing of Conflans from Brest as to leave little doubt but that there was a perfect understanding on the subject, between the Government of France and the Roman Catholic party in Ireland. Although the victory of Admiral Hawke put an end to their hopes at that time, the system was carried on in various ways, till we found a ramification of it under the term of Defenders, parading the Midland and some of the Northern counties and engaged chiefly in Armagh and Tyrone with the Protestants, who were called "Peep of Day Boys." To this last-named body I have never been able to trace anything like systematic affiliation.

One of the first open demonstrations of hostility on the part of the Romanists or Defenders was on the 12th July, 1791 or 92 - I forget which (1) - when a number of them well armed, with a white flag, etc., took post in an old and remarkably strong fort called Lisnagade, near Scarva, in County Down, with a view to prevent the Protestants from celebrating the day as usual with a procession. The Protestants, however, being apprised of their intention some days before made due preparation. An old blacksmith, James Spence, who still lives near me and with whom I have frequently conversed upon the subject, has told me that his Father who then lived at Cordrain, a place near Tandragee, purchased two guns for his sons to go to the Battle and thither they went.

Lisnagade fort is a circular area of considerable extent, thickly planted with trees and surrounded by a triple range of entrenchments and fosses, having but one entrance which was blockaded. On the approach of the Protestants, they were fired upon from the fort but, making a bold dash at it and taking advantage of the ditches near it to creep up and fire, the

Romanist party fled towards Loughbrickland, leaving some of their wounded behind. The Protestants were prevented from following up their victory by the arrival of a magistrate and a company of regulars who had been sent for in aid of the Civil Power, but arrived too late to prevent collision. Till then there was not a union of Protestants and this the other parties seem to have taken full advantage of.

There seems to have been at this period a great laxity of civil discipline in the country. The Constabulary was a nullity. A set of bog-bailiffs, game-keepers, and old hangers on of the County gentlemen received eight pounds a year each from the County under the application of Constables. Among these (?) the sole rivalry seemed to be who would do least for his hire. They were in general low profligate characters, a jest rather than a terror to evil doers. In point of activity their worships of the Commission (2) were with a few exceptions of little more service than their satellites.

The Magistrate if he had time heard complaints about broken heads and by his own fireside when brought before him crime was occasionally punished but little or no time was taken in the way of prevention - of course, I speak in a general way, for there were several exceptions.

The Defenders now waxed bold, a system of waylaying Protestants prevailed, none of them could return late particularly if alone from fair or market. But the most daring demonstration of any in those days was the tongue cutting outrage upon the family of Barclay, the schoolmaster, near Forkhill. This spoke the real spirit by which Romanism was (?) and exhibited the means by which she determined to carry her point.

The Protestants had the advantage of being better armed than their enemies, this rendered their (?) comparatively safe, whatever their persons might be when abroad. The arms of the old Volunteer Force remained in the country and to appropriate these to themselves now became the great object of the Defenders. The Protestant district lying between Loughgall and Richhill was fixed upon as the field for action in the disarming way upon a bold and more extensive scale than had hitherto been entered on here. About Monday, the 14th September, 1795, the Defenders began to rendezvous in small parties from Tyrone, Monaghan and Louth and the upper parts of Armagh. By Thursday, the 17th, a considerable number had assembled and posted themselves in an old fort or entrenchment on the summit of a commanding hill named Tullymore, about a mile and a half from the village of Loughgall, being supplied with provisions partly from the goodwill of the R. Catholics in the vicinity and in some degree by the instrumentality of foraging parties regularly sent out on that duty; they were well furnished with arms and ammunition and the story goes that some of the Clare Militia, a company of which lay in Portadown, were actively engaged in making cartridges for their service. The Protestants' houses were not so easy a prey as was anticipated. They also congregated from various quarters and took up a position on an eminence in the townland of Grangemore, equal in height to that on which the other party was posted and scarcely a musket shot from it, in the valley which separated the hills and at a place where four roads meet was a small cluster of houses called "The Diamond," a name since the events of that time famous in provincial records. The opposing parties kept up a desultory fire at each other, but at such a respectful distance that I believe no casualty took place on either side.

On Monday, the 14th, I had accompanied my Father and Mother and some other friends in a party to Belfast. We returned on Thursday, the 17th, and by the way heard reports of what was going forward - various and magnified as usual. At this time my father was adding to his dining room which occasioned the stripping of a considerable quantity of lead from the roof of the house. On the night of Thursday, the 17th, a carpenter's apprentice, Thomas Macan, and I made free with the best part of the lead and sat up nearly the entire night casting it into bullets of different sizes which Macan found means of having conveyed to the Belligerents of our side the next day - many of whom had gone from the townland of Bleary in the County Down, a district densely populated with stout Protestants, of a character somewhat lawless, owing in great measure to its localities, being secluded and nearly impassable for want of roads. These deficiencies have long since been remedied and there were not to be found more loyal fellows anywhere than the "Bleary Boys" proved themselves in the Rebellion of 1798.

By the afternoon of Friday, the 18th, the Defenders had discovered that they were in the wrong box and that the better part of valour was discretion and their commander, one Donnelly, distinguished by the Nomme De Guerre of "Switcher," became the more ready to accede to terms of truce which were entered into by Mr. Joseph Atkinson of Crowhill on the one side and Mr. Trainor, a popish priest, on the other.

On Saturday it was agreed that hostilities should cease and both parties withdraw to their homes. This was fulfilled by the great body of Protestants and by many of the Popish party also, but during Sunday, the 20th, a considerable reinforcement, chiefly of Defenders from Tyrone, joined the latter. These newcomers spurned at the idea of any(*thing*) like truce or treaty and resolved not to return home empty handed. Accordingly on Monday morning, the 21st, they poured down from their position on Tullymore (or Faughart as it is sometimes called) upon the little hamlet of the Diamond - the principal object of their attack being the house of a farmer named Winter. Luckily the Protestants had got some information of the arrival of this party and of their hostile disposition, which induced many of them to suspend their return home. The demonstration on Tullymore being conveyed to the body, they marched rapidly back to their position on Grangemore, where they arrived just in time to see the attack made on Winter's house by the Defenders, upon whom they instantly opened a heavy and well directed fire. Their position offered them many advantages; from the brow of the hill, which is very steep, they would fire with cool and steady aim at the swarms of Defenders, who were in a manner cooped up in the valley and presented an excellent mark for their shot. The affair was of brief duration. The Defenders, completely entrapped, made off leaving a number killed and wounded on the spot. The exact number who fell on the occasion I have never been able to ascertain; from those whom I saw carried off on cars that day and from the bodies found afterwards by the reapers in the cornfields along the line of their flight, I am inclined to think that not less than thirty may have lost their lives. Rumour, of course, more than quadrupled this number, but I rather imagine I am nearer the mark than her ladyship. Such was the far famed "Diamond Fight".

(Then follows a sermon on 1st Romans v 12)

Immediately after the battle and on the field of actions measures were adopted for the formation of a defensive association of Protestants, and these were carried into effect as far as a commencement went, in the house of James Sloan, in the village of Loughgall, about two miles from the Diamond. Sloan acted as Secretary and issued what were called "numbers," a kind of rude warrant for holding lodges. The first ten or a dozen were drawn for and No. 1 fell to the lot of the Dyan Lodge held in the petty hamlet in Tyrone, adjoining the Blackwater and about midway between

Benburb and Caledon. This beginning of the Orange Organisation, with the pass words and regulations, have, through the medium of parliamentary reports, become matters of historical record. A reference to those reports does away this necessity of my going over the same ground again, at least in anything like a general way. I shall, therefore, confine myself to those particulars in which *pars magna fui.* (**3**) The great roads leading from Tandragee to Lurgan and from Banbridge to Portadown after meeting and crossing each other at Drumlin Hill run parallel for the distance of about a mile. They are connected near the gate of Carrick (**4**) by a narrow road called the long Lonan, in those days not only very solitary from there not being an inhabited house throughout its length but also labouring under a bad character from the superstition of the neighbours. Many a time have I shuddered in the nursery at hearing tales of the black dog and the man without a head who were supposed to be its nightly perambulators. He was accounted a hardy child who would venture to traverse it alone after the day was completely closed. The case is altered now. It is bordered by five or six comfortable farm house and many a night I have heard it made vocal, delightfully vocal, by the children of my singing class returning from their lesson of psalmody and praise at the school of Hacknahay. But to return - the first house in this lonan and had been just built and covered in but the walls had not been perforated for the windows so that all was as dark within as any conspirator could desire. The proverb says "Walls have ears". I can only say that if these had any such organs they must have resembled those of a Newfoundland dog after a duck hunt for they were dripping wet. In this dreaded land and within these damp walls did our first Orange Lodge in this quarter hold its meetings and, then, on the first night of its formation did I and sundry others join it. This house was built by Alexr. Patten and is the same now occupied by Thomas England on the face of the hill in the Lonan. It was a scene not unworthy of the pen of a Scott or the pencil of Salvator Rosa to view the assemblage of men, young and old collected on these occasions, as far as could be seen by the light of a few small candles, seated on heaps of sods or rude blocks of wood, more standing in various attitudes, most of them armed with guns of every age and calibre, long "Queen Anne's" and pistols of low degree to which the term of patent safety might be applied with greater truth than to many of the coaches which now bear it in England, in as much as rust and antiquity had blighted the spring of their days into utter incapacity to strike fire. There was a stern solemnity in the reading the lesson from Scripture and administering the oath to the newly admitted brethren which was calculated to produce a deep impression and did so. There was a fixed steady fierce devotedness to the cause which brought them together, which showed their adhesion to it was the result of deliberation, not of impulse, of principle, not of passion. They did not rush blindly or under the influence of mere example to the Order, they had pondered the matter and had become convinced of the absolute necessity of a defensive union among Protestants. This feeling was in no small degree excited by men (sundry of whom were in existence in the country) of very advanced age who had in the early period of their lives lived with those who had been at a still more remote period witnesses of or partakers in the war of the Revolution of 1688 and who had heard from the lips of those patriarchs of the Boyne and Aughrim of the suffering which had driven them to the field in arms.

One of these ancient worthies resided on Carrick Estate. His name was William Lutton, a most respectable old man. He was born in 1710, only 20 years after the Battle of the Boyne so that at 20 he might have met and conversed with many who had been stout young fellows from 25 to 30 in that memorable action and at the time of his conversing with them, men of clear intellect of from 60 to 70 years of age. Often and often have I sat by his side listening to his tales of those "Boys of Boyne" as he used to call them. He died in 1802 aged 92.

The farmers and linen dealers in the country whose business called them to the markets and sometimes detained them there until a lateish hour, were not slow in availing themselves of an association which promised them protection upon those occasions. In fact matters had come to such a pass that no Protestant who ventured upon the road alone after nightfall was safe and neighbours were obliged to make parties and wait for each other on Fair and Market days. Upon this state of things the victory of the Diamond and the foundation of Orange Lodges had a speedy and beneficial effect.

Very few of the resident gentry of the Country joined us in the first instance. Of those few were my old friend, Joseph Atkinson, Esq., already mentioned; the Revd. George Maunsile,(sic. Maunsell) **(5)** of Drumcree, afterwards Dean of Leighlin; Captain Clarke, of Summer Island, and soon after the young Verners of Church Hill. Old Mr. Verner never joined as an affiliated member, though he took a great interest in the proceedings of the Association. That excellent man, the venerable and beloved Viscount Northland, of Dungannon, was, I believe, the first nobleman who fostered by his patronage the infant Institution. Mr. Brownlow, of Lurgan, who had succeeded his distinguished father in his estate and in the representation of the County in 1794, also took an early interest in our welfare and become one of us, as did old Major Waring, of Waringstown, a veteran of George II's wars.

In the month of October I was taken to Dublin to enter College and my father having removed for the winter months into the city of Armagh I escaped being in any sort a witness to those scenes which took place in the County about that period and which cannot be referred to without pain, exaggerated as was the account of them.

Happy had it been for the Protestant name if the Protestants had content with the defeat of their enemies at the Diamond and the formation of a protective society. Unhappily it was not so, a spirit of vengeance and retaliation had sunk too deeply in many of their minds to be thus easily satisfied. Many it is true had a long account of wrong to suffer in this eagerness after which they totally overlooked the divine declaration: "Vengeance is mine, I will repay, saith the Lord," and in an evil hour they took into their own hands the mode of payment. A determination was expressed of driving from this quarter of the Country of its entire Roman Catholic population. It is true a great proportion of these had taken an active part as Defenders and Persecutors of Protestants; still there were many who were "quiet in the land," and had taken no share in such proceedings, but revenge, like love, is blind.

(There now follows Pages 242 - 244)

This frightful state of things lasted for nearly two months. The number of families driven from their homes has been variously stated; some have rated it as high as 500 but from all the enquiries I have been able to make I am led conscientiously to believe that 180 would be nearer the mark. Too many, God knows, yet still far short of what it has suited the purposes of Party since to assert.

The storm, however, passed over, a paralysed magistracy resumed its functions, troops were sent into the country, but the truth is that in proportion as the Orange organisation progressed disorder declined. The Masters of Lodges took an active and proper part, bad spirits were checked, the advice of steady men prevailed and the non-admission of any known "wrecker" into an Orange Lodge had a powerful effect in put(*ing*) an end to further outrages on the part of the lower classes of Protestants.

EDITORS NOTES

(1) R.M. Sibbett in "Orangeism in Ireland and Throughout the Empire" gives the date of the Battle of Lisnagade as 12th July 1791. Local tradition has the date as 1783. This is supported by the late J.C. Patterson who quotes several contemporary accounts, by Rev. M.W. Dewar in "The Scarva Story"; and by George Patton in "Scarva". David W. Millar in "Peep of Day Boys and Defenders" is incorrect in quoting a letter to the Earl of Charlemont by John Moore as giving 1789 as the date. The letter was written in 1789 but it refers to past events without quoting a date. Col. Blacker was writing about 50 years later in 1836.

(2) "Their worships of the Commission": the local magistrates.

(3) I.e., in which I played a large part.

(4) I.e., the Colonel's own Carrickblacker estate.

(5) 'Maunsell' is the spelling in the Parish Records. Aiken McClelland in his "Formation of the Orange Order" on page 11 spells it as "Maunsel" and adds the footnote: "Maunsel was Rector of Drumcree 1781-1804". Hereward Senior in his "Orangeism in Ireland and Britain 1795-1836" (1966) Page 20 has a double error by stating: "Rev. George Marshall of Dromore".

BIOGRAPHICAL NOTE ON

COLONEL ROBERT H. WALLACE
1860-1929

Robert Hugh Wallace was a son of the late William Nevin Wallace D.L. of Myra Castle on the shores of Strangford Lough, on the Downpatrick side of Castle Ward Estate. He was born at the family home on 14th December, 1860 and educated at Harrow and Oxford where he graduated in law in 1883. He was called to the Bar in 1886. On the death of his father he became head of the firm of Messrs. Hugh Wallace and Co. Solicitors, Belfast and Downpatrick.

He was commissioned as a 2nd Lieutenant in the 5th Battalion Royal Irish Rifles (South Down Militia) in 1879 with which he was associated for 34 years. He was promoted to the command of the Battalion as Lt. Col. in 1899, a position he held for 15 years.

In the South African War 1899 - 1902, he served with distinction, being awarded the C.B., the Queen's Medal with 5 clasps and mentioned in Dispatches. He was noted for his courtesy and chivalry to a beaten foe and received the cordial thanks of General De Wet for kindness to himself and family.

In 1914, he was recalled to the Colours and raised and trained the 17th Battalion Royal Irish Rifles. He then took over command of 19th Battalion till he retired due to poor health in January 1918 when he was awarded the C.B.E. He was the author of the song "The South Down Militia" beginning "I belong to a noble regiment, whose deeds are often told".

As a young man he joined Eldon L.O.L. No. 7 and in 1903 succeeded Colonel Edward Saunderson as County Grand Master of Belfast, at a time of dissension within the Order. He held this position till 1921 and was instrumental in founding the Belfast Orange Widows Fund. For part of this time he was also Grand Secretary of the Grand Orange Lodge (1903 - 1910) and Grand President of the Grand Orange Council of the World (1909 - 1912). During the home rule crisis, he played an active part in the Ulster Volunteer Force.

He married Caroline Wilhelmina Twigg of Cookstown and had a son and three daughters. Tragically, his son was drowned in a yachting accident in 1930.

He worshipped, up until the Sunday before he died, in Down Cathedral where, in 1931, the Masonic Province of Down placed a memorial window depicting Hiram, King of Tyre.

Colonel Robert H. Wallace, C.B., C.B.E., D.L.

INTRODUCTION TO
THE WALLACE PAPERS

The papers, deposited for safe keeping with the Public Record Office by the family of the late Colonel Wallace, have been divided into Military papers, Unionist papers, Masonic papers, Church papers (Mainly Down Cathedral) and Orange papers. The main element of the latter are two hand written exercise books which are part of an unfinished, unedited and unpublished History of the Orange Order. Tragically, the first volume of nine chapters and 100 pages has been lost.

The first surviving volume commences half way through Chapter 9 and runs to the end of Chapter 16, containing 110 pages. The last volume is incomplete and has only 3 chapters and 59 pages.

It would appear that the Colonel had been working on his script for some time, making alterations here and there, adding footnotes and chapter headings. The handwriting is beautiful, clear and neat, using a very fine nib. Occasionally, where two S's occur together, he uses the long S for the first.

The history is dated 1899 which was the year that the Colonel's Regiment, the famous South Down Militia, embarked for the South African War. Perhaps the writing was put aside, to be completed when time permitted, but time ran out, and we must be grateful that two very valuable volumes have survived.

The task of writing the history of the period after 1798, when Grand Lodge removed to Dublin, was facilitated by newspapers which began to publish details of its meetings and resolutions. The Colonel had access to many newspaper cuttings from an unknown source but dated back to 1797. Thus the last volume is interspersed with such cuttings which add greatly to its authenticity. He obviously intended to continue the account as the last page contains cuttings from a newspaper dated 1820, although his history had not yet reached the year 1799.

Probably, as time went on, the Colonel was glad to hand over the task to another Orange historian who had more time available. In the introduction to the 2nd Edition of "Orangeism", Bro. R.M. Sibbett writes, "Over a decade later, when the present writer undertook to compile this "History of Orangeism" Bro. Colonel Wallace placed at his disposal all the writings of Bro. Lilburn in his possession." The first edition of Bro. Sibbett's work appeared in 1914. Perhaps thereafter the Colonel thought that his work was superfluous.

In the opinion of the Education Committee, his work is of such a quality and fills so many gaps in our knowledge, that after almost another 100 years its importance is enhanced rather than diminished. Like good wine it has been kept till the last.

These Papers are presented with only the minimum amount of editing. We have favoured a uniformity of spelling, except in the case of older forms of spelling, which have been maintained and also in the case of quotations which Colonel Wallace makes from other sources. Some chapter headings have been introduced to assist the reader with the content of the Papers. The footnotes form part of the Papers except where indicated.

HISTORY OF THE ORANGE ORDER:

THE FORMATIVE YEARS, 1795 - 1798
By
Col. R.H. Wallace, C.B., C.B.E., D.L.

The Diamond leaders return to Loughgall

In due time, according to arrangement, the Diamond leaders met again in Sloan's house(*), and each reported the result of the inquiry he had made. Without exception, the reports were in favour of union among Protestants; but the form and name of the organisation had still to be determined. James Wilson was the best informed and most experienced man in the company; and, after having fully and thoughtfully discussed the subject, bearing in mind the opposition excited by the whinney hill meetings,(**) and the difficulties that they might have to encounter in connection with the new arrangements, it was unanimously resolved to adopt the Orange Boys Society as the working model; to admit Protestants only to membership; and, in compliment to the memory of the Prince of Orange, to call the proposed organisation the Orange Society, the initiated to be known as Orange Men.

As yet no Warrants had been prepared; it was impossible to draw up forms authorising Lodges to be held till the preliminaries mentioned were gone through. Even when these matters were settled a considerable time necessarily elapsed before anything akin to a Warrant could be provided. Meanwhile, it was agreed to imitate the example set in regard to making inquiry; and, therefore, slips of paper were again issued bearing a number, the name of the person to whom a Warrant might be issued, and the place of meeting. One of these documents was handed by Col. Blacker to the Select Committee on Orange Lodges, and here is a copy of it:-

*(*) The first meeting in Sloan's house, immediately after the Battle of the Diamond, is specifically mentioned on page 147f under the heading "First Organised issue of Warrants". (**Editor**)*

*(**) This meeting of the "Orange Boys" held in the townland of Colrevog near Moy, had been arranged by James Wilson in 1794. (**Editor**)*

> No. eighty-nine Timakeel, July 7th, 1796
>
> James Sloan
> To be renewed in the name of Daniel Bulla, Portadown District(*)

Another of these unpretentious documents was seen by Mr. Edward Rogers of Armagh and may be reproduced:-

> No. one hundred and seventeen, Armagh, August 14th, 1796
>
> James Sloan.

With this Number is supplied a rude seal having an equestrian figure of King William surrounded by the words King and Constitution, and bearing the initials J.S. Each slip of paper cost the person to whom it was addressed £1.2.9, the old Irish guinea. These slips of paper, however, were not Warrants properly so called.

They merely guaranteed that the holders might receive Warrants when the distribution took place, while in the meantime they were empowered to form Orange Clubs, or Societies. The first regular issue of Warrants occurred in 1798. There is no record of what happened in Daniel Bulla's case, although No. 89 is registered in Portadown District, renewed in May, 1824; and, as regards No. 117, it was issued in 1798, without a Master's name in the register, and in 1823 was renewed in Newtownhamilton District.

There is no doubt those who met in Sloan's parlour, and others also, were authorised to form Orange Societies; and, although the organisation was imperfect, the work went on rapidly in Armagh and in the various Counties throughout Ulster. The rule was "first come first served", and it left no room for a feeling of jealousy or a charge of favouritism. By virtue of his position, in relation to the Orange Boys, James Wilson demanded and obtained No.1, while for the reason already stated No.2 was allotted to Derryscollop. It is said that the man who received No.3 was so elated with his prize that he hurried off without bidding good bye to anyone, and when he reached the Blackwater, the ferry boat not being convenient, he plunged into the river as he was, and swam to the other side, he was so eager to convey the news to his comrades.

(*) Daniel Bulla was District Master of Portadown. The present D.M. (1899) is Mr. William John Lock an active and efficient officer.

26

The lightning speed with which Orangeism spread proves its adaptability to the wants of loyal men in the period. Touching No.1 having found a home in Tyrone, instead of in the County of Armagh, there was much controversy at the time and for years afterwards. Diamond Dan believed that he ought to have been the possessor, and refused to take out a Number until several had been sold and circulated. It was alleged that James Wilson succeeded by a "fluke", but there was no "fluke" in the business. Mr. Edward Rogers, as an Armagh Orangeman and Grand Secretary to the County Orange Lodge, could not be reconciled to No.1 being in the Dyan, and he accounted for it in this way:-

"A few days after the struggle at the Diamond, some persons from that locality came to Loughgall, for the purpose of procuring from Sloan the necessary authority for admitting members into their Lodge. Being in his garden at the time, Sloan directed them to the village to procure writing materials. During their absence, James Wilson, on a similar errand, arrived from the Dyan. On being informed that there was neither pen nor ink, he at once replied, "If that be all, I can provide against that, and 'tis best, for the first Orange Warrant should not be written by anything made by the hand of man;" and, taking a sprig from a tree of hyssop which grew in the garden, he handed it, together with the cover of a letter, to Sloan, who, being taken aback by the novelty of the proceeding, incautiously signed the paper, thus establishing the claim of "The Dyan Men" to a number which, by right, should never have left the vicinity of the field of victory. When the men who had gone to the village returned and found what had been done, nothing could exceed their disappointment, and finally they refused to take a Warrant. Others, more fortunate, stepped in, and these poor fellows now rejoice in the possession of No.118."

The explanation is ingenious, but inconsistent with existing conditions at the time. Sloan's house was in the village, and there was no need to go into the village to procure writing materials, because if such things were to be found anywhere it could be in a public house, especially in one to which the linen drapers resorted for the purpose of paying for the webs they had bought in the open market. The legend of the sprig of hyssop was connected with the formation of the first Lodge of Orange Boys, although hyssop does not usually grow on whinney hills. Moreover, the plant was not grown in Sloan's garden at any time, certainly not in the neighbourhood of the summer house, which was constructed of common sallows, to the growth of which the dampness of the locality was favourable. Even if the sprig of hyssop had been available, it must have been dipped into ink to enable Sloan to sign his name on the cover of a letter alleged to have been handed to him by Wilson. The story cannot be reconciled to facts. Sloan held his levees in the garden; his visitors at the time were numerous, and could not be accommodated in the parlour, which was a small room, about nineteen feet in length and ten in breadth, while the walls are some three feet broad, according to the custom of the age, the idea being to enable occupiers to resist the assaults from without, then so common.

Another version of the story of Number One was supplied by an old Orangeman named Woods, who lived in Loughgall. He said nothing about the sprig of hyssop; but he maintained that the Dyan Men got the number by "chance". The "chance" occurred when there was a clamour of many voices demanding Warrants; and the only atonement that could be made to the disappointed Armagh Men was to allot to their County Numbers 2, 3 and 4, Woods himself being the first Worshipful Master of Number 4. The vicissitudes of time and circumstances have deprived the County of Armagh of 3 and 4. There is reason to believe that the success of the enterprise was menaced by the conflict of opinion in regard to Number One. Dan Winter and his neighbours claimed it, and refused to take out any other, which accounts for the lateness of the Diamond Warrant. But Wilson and his Orange Boys were in the field, and could have interrupted the progress of the effort. Therefore, prudent wisdom prevailed, and it was resolved not to attempt to undo what had been done. Two Orange organisations at the beginning might have proved fatal to the defensive object the Protestants had in view, and the North of Ireland, indeed all Ireland, would have had cause to regret the misfortune. The teaching of experience is not favourable to more than one Orange Society. It was well therefore, that Sloan nipped division in the bud.

Little need be said in relation to the Dyan Men having secured their prize by "chance". Woods was not in the summer house with Wilson, and he merely repeated the story as he had heard it. His words are esteemed, although the Dyan Men never did, and never will, accept them. They say the Warrant reached them by right of succession to the Number One they were willing to have cancelled. Furthermore, they allege that the sprig of hyssop was used by the Orange Boys on the whinney hill, and was among the emblems present at the initiation of members; and that there was no "chance" at all in the proceedings. There is no doubt there were Lodges of Orange Boys, and the prime Lodge sat at the Dyan. Hence, assigning Number One to that locality was nothing more than a renewal of the Warrant already there in working order. Sloan had cognisance of these facts; and it is no tribute to his memory to state that he was caught napping. He was a wide awake man; his house was the resort of Protestants; it was in the village of Loughgall; and it is absurd that it did not obtain writing materials. In the absence of the envoys where did Wilson get the ink? The sprig of hyssop must have been dipped into ink; and if Wilson brought ink with him he would also have brought a pen. The only rational mode of accounting for Number One being at the Dyan is, that James Wilson would not have dissolved his Orange Boys Society on any other terms; and James Sloan was too sagacious to encourage two Orange organisations. We can now look back and admire his wisdom.

In its infancy the Orange system had to struggle against many difficulties. It had been conceived and brought forth by humble men, who sang its first lullaby. It is disparagement to the gentry to say that at first they stood aloof, and began to form Protestant Associations in cities and towns and villages and rural districts. These Associations worked well for a time; but there was no tie on the members, most of whom acted according to what was right in their own eyes. Moreover, some of the Associations could not be controlled. There was nothing exclusive in the membership; the doors were open to all who professed to be loyal to the interests of Protestantism. the intention was good, but proved to be impracticable. What loyal Protestants wanted was not to be found in either the mixed or Protestant Associations; and it was to be found in the Orange system. Therefore, it spread with the rapidity of lightning through Armagh and the other Northern counties. Every step taken by Sloan and his friends was attended with difficulties; but they held on to their purpose.

Their greatest trouble was to give form to the organisation - to provide something simple enough for humble men to understand, and strong enough to keep them together. Day by day the founders met in council; and in every meeting the dominant sentiment was that, if the star lighted in the Dyan(*) was to receive brilliancy from the victory at the Diamond and the deliberations in Loughgall, the Society should be secret and be limited to

(*) This relates to an incident in Benburb on 24th June 1794, proir to the Whinny Hill meeting. See R.M. Sibbett Page 267. (Editor)

Protestants, who would require to submit to certain tests to qualify for membership.

At length it was arranged to hold a general meeting in private on a day named. Immediately after the Battle of the Diamond, the Government sent a party of soldiers to Loughgall. They were in that town as we have seen when Mr. Richard Jephson wrote to Lord Charlemont, under date October 9, 1795. Among the troops was a company of the Dublin militia, commanded by Captain Gifford,(*) who was then and there admitted into the Orange Society, to which he subsequently rendered valuable service. Captain Gifford was present at the general meeting, and so also were Colonel Sheldrake and Captain Cramp, who are said to have belonged to an English regiment, and may have been on a tour of inspection. The names of Sheldrake and Cramp were given to the late Mr. Charles J. Nicholson, of Crannagil House, near Loughgall, by his father, who was born ten years before the Battle of the Diamond, and died in 1875, in his ninetieth year. The stirring scenes of the time made a lasting impression on the young lad's mind, and thenceforward during a long and useful life he watched and noted the current of events. His words were confirmed, if confirmation were necessary, by an old man named Irwin - in his 87th year when his opinion was asked - who was for many years Master of No.5, sitting in Kinnego, in the County of Armagh. Immediately the question was put to him he named Colonel Sheldrake as one of the officers, but thought the other was Colonel Elson. There were, however, two English military officers in Loughgall in the early days of Orangeism, and they assisted in organising the system, to which they took kindly, receiving valuable help from Captain Gifford, who rose to eminence as a member of the Grand Orange Lodge of Ireland.

Early Difficulties

Although Number One had gone to the County of Tyrone, it was agreed, by all concerned, that, in compliment to the County of Armagh, the first regular Lodge meeting should be held in Sloan's in Loughgall, which was attended by James Wilson and a few of his friends. As long as they kept within doors there was nothing to fear, being quite competent to take care of themselves. Still, as regards initiation, there were serious difficulties in

(*) *Captain John Gifford became Deputy Grand Master in 1806 and Acting Grand Master of Ireland 1814 - 1819. (**Editor**)*

30

the way. at the beginning the gentry were not friendly to the new order of affairs, preferring more general Associations. Naturally enough the proprietors of the country wished to maintain control over their tenantry and the local executive authorities. At that time Mr. Savage Hall was High Sheriff of the County of Armagh, and, in compliance with a requisition, he convened a meeting of magistrates, which was held in Armagh Court House on the 19th of October, 1795. It was unanimously felt that something should be done to preserve the peace, which was disturbed by mobs of vicious and disorderly persons, who assembled in considerable bodies, attacked the houses of well disposed inhabitants, and plundered their arms, money and other property.

These mobs, no matter by what name they might be known, were to be brought to condign punishment. Moreover, the magistrates present bound themselves, collectively and individually, to assist in preserving the tranquility of their several districts. For this laudable purpose they called upon all loyal citizens to join with them, promising to observe secrecy in regard to membership, and to reward those who tendered public or private information against offenders. In addition, convenient places were appointed for the magistrates to administer the Oath of Allegiance to all who should voluntarily come forward to testify their attachment to the King and Constitution. Those who took the Oath were to have certificates to that effect if they required them. It was further resolved that the magistrates, Constables, Sub-Constables and other Peace Officers, should be on the alert to seize arms, ammunition and all kinds of offensive weapons found in the possession of persons not qualified to have them; to prosecute those who openly carried arms contrary to law; and to enforce the prescribed penalty against selling gunpowder against license. Having settled these preliminaries the meeting adjourned.

Mixed Associations

On the 26th of October the magistrates re-assembled in Armagh Court House, and the second and final step was taken in regard to the formation of Mixed Associations. On this occasion there were present, Lord Gosford, Governor of the County; Sir Capel Molyneux, Bart.; Messrs. Robert C. Cope, Michael Obins, Hugh Hamilton, Nicholas A. Cope, William Clarke, John Ogle, Robert Bernard Sparrow, James A. Hamilton, Joshua McGeough, Joseph Atkinson, Robert Livingston, Kennick Cope, William Bisset, Daniel Kelly and William Sodge.

The County was then in a very disturbed state, requiring the immediate interference of all lovers of law and order. Accordingly it was resolved that, as bodies of armed men still continue to parade through different parts of the County both by day and by night, committing great outrages and disturbing the peaceable inhabitants, all gentlemen of property be recommended, without loss of time, either by themselves or their agents, to bring their tenants together, and require them to engage in the most solemn manner, that they will keep the peace with all their neighbours and fellow subjects, and to their utmost avoid doing injury to their persons or property, and never to join with or encourage any party of men who meet for any purpose tending to disturb the peace of the country. The following form of a voluntary oath was recommended:-

"I, A.B., do freely and willingly swear, that I will keep the peace with all my neighbours and fellow-subjects, and not designedly injure any of them, except it be in my own defence, and that I will never join with, or encourage, any party of men whatever who meet together for purposes whereby the peace of the country may be violated. And this oath I take in the fear of God and in the true faith of a Christian."

Before separating a subscription was opened to carry out the objects proposed, and handsome sums were contributed. Lord Gosford, the Lord Primate, and Lord Charlemont gave £100 each; Sir Capel Molyneux, Messrs. William Richardson, William Brownlow, Savage Hall, Robert C. Cope, Joshua McGeough, Robert Sparrow, N.A. Cope, Kennick Cope, James Johnston, William Clarke, John Godley, £50 each; Mr. Robert Maxwell, Rev. Hugh Hamilton Messrs. Michael Obins, James Ashmur, 20 guineas each; Messrs. James A. Hamilton, Samuel Close, Arthur J. Macan, Robert Livingston, Rev. William Bisset, Messrs. Daniel Kelly, Joseph Atkinson, Robert Best, Rev. William Lodge, Messrs. Peter Gervis and William Irwin, £20 each.

This movement was purely defensive; and, while showing that something was required to check the turbulence that prevailed, it was very likely due in part to the arrangements made in Sloan's to test public opinion in regard to the form of organisation needed. The magisterial meeting included Whigs and Tories, and the scope of the Association was too much enlarged to produce the desired effect. After what had occurred at the Diamond it was impossible to bring Protestants and Roman Catholics together, and to set the latter against their co-religionists, the Defenders, who were keeping alive the ferment in the country.

The Association had little influence in the direction intended except in the towns, and even there certain threats about Connaught or a worse place were inscribed on the doors and in public thoroughfares, to be read by all men. There was too much of the upper class in the enterprise, and the masses, the Protestant farmers and linen manufacturers, stood aloof. What they wanted was an organisation formed and fashioned by their own hands, in harmony with their own ideas, and outside the control of landed proprietors, agents, bailiffs, baronial constables, and all the rest.

Hence, the Mixed Associations failed, especially in the rural districts, whose inhabitants were in most need of protection. Two examples may be quoted. On Monday December 14th, two young men were fired at between Armagh and Richill. When they reached the latter they gave information, and fifty soldiers with an officer marched to the house in which the murderous gang - a party of Defenders - had concealed themselves. They refused to surrender, and the house was set on fire; four of the inmates were killed on the spot, and fourteen of the survivors were brought as prisoners to Armagh gaol. Next morning two men were fired at near Tandragee by fellows who had previously robbed four pedlars, two of whom were stabbed with bayonets. The Defenders continued their outrages, plundering the houses of Protestants, houghing their cattle, and destroying other property. On the other hand, the Peep of Day Boys took revenge on the enemy at every opportunity.

The County was both disturbed and alarmed. Therefore, Lord Gosford convened another meeting of magistrates, which was held in Armagh December 26, 1795. There were present Sir Capel Molyneux; Messrs William Richardson, William Brownlow, A.J. Macan (Sovereign of Armagh), Robert B. Sparrow, Alexander Thomas Stewart, Michael Obins; Rev. Hugh Hamilton; Mr. Joseph McGeough, Mr. James Verner; Rev. Richard Allott; Mr. Stewart Blacker, Mr. John Reilly, Mr. Samuel Close, Mr. John Ogle, Mr. William Clarke, Mr. C.M. Warburton; Rev. William Lodge, Rev William Bisset; Mr. Thomas Quin, Mr. Owen O'Callaghan, Mr. John Maxwell, Mr. William Irwin, Mr. James Harden, Mr. James Lawson, Mr. William Barker, and Mr. Robert Livingston. This array of names shows that the County was thoroughly represented in the assembly. They were all gentlemen of integrity and of good social position. Some were Whigs, other Tories, and one a Roman Catholic; while Mr. Hamilton, Mr. Warburton and Mr. Bisset were of such reputation in the Church that they were promoted to the Episcopal Bench, and filled respectively the office of Bishops in the Sees of Ossory, Limerick, and Raphoe.

Lord Gosford's alleged speech

But the significance of the meeting is not derived from its constitution. There was nothing remarkable in the Governor of the County convoking the Justices to consider what was best to be done to arrest outrage in his and their jurisdictions. The remarkable thing in connection with the business was a speech alleged to have been delivered by his Lordship, and subsequently printed as a hand bill, which was circulated throughout the County and in other parts of Ireland, exciting much controversy then and since.

The speech was a favourite weapon in the hands of the enemies of Orangeism. Henry Grattan was the first to give to the document an interpretation which it did not bear; and his sympathisers and successors followed in his wake, the rivalry being to divert plain language with the view to affixing guilt upon innocent men. Plowden, Samson, Madden, and minor writers, have made the worst possible use of a document whose authorship has never been proved, and with which there is good reason to believe Lord Gosford had no connection. Still, in every part of the British Islands, and wherever Orangeism appeared, the Speech was produced and hurled at the Orangemen. Here is a copy of the document, which was addressed to the magistrates present, not to the Grand Jury of Armagh as stated by Mr. Plowden -

"Gentlemen, having requested your presence here today, it becomes my duty to state the grounds upon which I thought it advisable to propose this meeting, and at the same time to submit to your consideration a plan, which occurs to me most likely to check the enormities which have already brought disgrace upon this County, and may soon reduce it into deep distress. It is no secret that a persecution, accompanied with all the circumstances of ferocious cruelty, which have in all ages distinguished that dreadful calamity, is now raging in this County. Neither age nor sex, nor even acknowledged innocence as to any guilt in the late disturbances, is sufficient to excite mercy, much less to afford protection.

"The only crime which the wretched objects of this ruthless persecution are charged with is a crime indeed of easy proof: it is simply a profession of the Roman Catholic faith, or an intimate connection with a person professing that faith. A lawless banditti have constituted themselves judges of this new species of delinquency, and the sentence they have pronounced is equally concise and terrible: it is nothing less than a confiscation of all property, and an immediate banishment. It would be extremely painful, and surely unnecessary, to detail the horrors that attend the execution of so wide and tremendous a proscription - a proscription that certainly exceeds, in the comparative number of those it consigns to ruin and misery, every example that ancient or modern history can supply; for where have we heard, or in what story of human cruelties have we read, of more than half the inhabitants of a populous County deprived at one blow of the means as well as of the fruits of their industry, and driven, in the midst of an inclement season, to seek a shelter for themselves and their helpless families where chance may guide them? This is no exaggerated picture of the horrid scenes now acting in the County; yet surely it is sufficient to awaken sentiments of indignation and compassion in the coldest bosom. These horrors, I say, are now acting, and acting with impunity. "The spirit of impartial justice (without which law is nothing better than an instrument of tyranny,) has for a time disappeared for a time in this County, and the supineness of the magistracy of Armagh is become a common topic of conversation in every corner of the kingdom. It is said, in reply, the Roman Catholics are dangerous. They may be so; they may be dangerous from their numbers, and still more dangerous from the unbounded views they have been encouraged to entertain; but I will venture to assert, without fear of contradiction, that upon those very grounds these terrible proceedings are not more contrary to humanity than they are to ,sound policy. It is to be lamented that no civil magistrate happened to be present with the military detachments on the night of the 21st instant; but I trust the suddenness of the occasion, the unexpected and instantaneous aggression on the part of the delinquents, will be universally admitted as a full vindication of the conduct of the officer and the party under his command. Gentlemen, I have the honour to hold a situation in this County which calls upon me to deliver my sentiments, and I do so without fear and without disguise.

"I am as true a Protestant as any gentleman in this room, or in this kingdom; I inherit a property which my family derived under a Protestant title, and with the blessing of God I will maintain that title to the utmost of my power; I will never consent to make a sacrifice of Protestant Ascendancy to Catholic claims, with whatever meanness they may be urged, or however spaciously or insidiously supported. Conscious of my sincerity in this public declaration, which I do not make unadvisedly, but as the result of mature deliberation, I defy the paltry insinuations that malice or party spirit may suggest. I know my own heart, and I should despise myself if, under any intimidation, I could close my eyes against such scenes as present themselves on every side, or shut my ears against the complaints of a persecuted people. I should be guilty of an unpardonable injustice to the feelings of gentlemen here present were I to say more on this subject. I have now acquitted myself to my conscience and my country."

The noble Lord then moved the following resolutions, which were unanimously adopted:-

"**1.** That it appears to this meeting that the County of Armagh is at this moment in a state of uncommon disorder; that the Roman Catholic inhabitants are grievously oppressed by lawless persons unknown, who attack and plunder their houses by night, and threaten them with instant destruction unless they immediately abandon their lands and habitations.

2. That a committee of magistrates be appointed to sit on Tuesdays and Saturdays in the chapter room in the town of Armagh, to receive information respecting all persons of whatever description who disturb the peace of this County.

3. That the instruction of the whole body of the magistracy to their committee shall be to use every legal means within their power to stop the progress of the persecution now carrying on, by an ungovernable mob, against the Roman Catholic inhabitants of this County.

4. That said committee, or any three of them, be empowered to expend any sum or sums of money for information or secret service, out of the fund subscribed by the gentlemen of this County.

5. That a meeting of the whole board of the magistracy be held every second Monday, at the house of Mr. Charles McReynolds, in the town of Armagh, to hear the reports of the committee, and to give such further instructions as the exigency of the times may require.

6. That offenders of every description in the present disturbances shall be prosecuted out of the fund subscribed by the gentlemen of this County. And to carry this resolution into effect, be it also resolved, that Mr. Arthur Irvine be appointed law agent to the magistracy."

In these documents, which testify to the desire of the Governor and Magistrates to maintain the peace of the County of Armagh, the whole armour of the assailants is exposed to public view; and, after all, there was nothing affecting the Orange Society, which had not then come into existence. The meeting was held on December 28, 1795, three months after the Battle of the Diamond, and it was an adjournment from other meetings in October, the first convened by the High Sheriff, within a month after the Battle, so that whoever may have been aimed at, the Orangemen could not have been intended, because there were no Orangemen at the time. This is an absolute matter of historic fact, excluding controversy. Neither in the speech alleged to have been delivered by Lord Gosford, nor in the resolutions adopted, was a solitary word uttered implicating Orange Boys or Orange Men.

It cannot be denied that tumult prevailed in certain parts of the County of Armagh, and that in these parts military forces were necessary to protect life and property. Soldiers were stationed in Loughgall, Richill, and in neighbouring towns, while some were billeted in the houses of Roman Catholics for defensive purposes. Such excitement, however, was general in Ireland at the time, and was ascribed to seditious movements on the one hand, and on the other to the circulation of immoral literature. The wave of revolution had spread from France over many countries, and the British Islands did not escape. The infamous works of Tom Paine were popular in Ireland, and had much to do in the demoralisation of society both in England and Ireland. Here is a specimen of the sentiments of the members of seditious societies in England -

"That the tyrants of England may be divided into several classes; that most fatal to the felicity of a country are governors of all descriptions, priests, soldiers, and lawyers."

Still worse were the aspersions hurled at the King, and the violent assault made upon our common Christianity. "We were perplexed," said the admirers of their deistical countryman, "with another description of tyranny - men who hallow the Divinity. The Books of Moses and of Christ answer to the cobweb Charters of State produced in support of pious fraud, and were never written by the men whose names they bear; those men had in all ages the defenders of despotism." In fact, the rights of all duly constituted authority were assailed, and efforts were made to destroy the social fabric.

To such a dangerous altitude had sedition risen in England that Proclamations were issued prohibiting the assemblage of crowds; and subsequently an Act was passed making it a penal offence for more than fifty persons to meet together, except convened by the Lord Lieutenant of a County, the *Custos Rotulorum* (Keeper of the Rolls), The Sheriff, two or more Justices of the Peace, or other recognised local authorities. The trials in England of persons arraigned for high treason sufficiently proved the design to invite the French to invade that country; and although Stone, who carried on his correspondence over the signature of Enots - his name transposed - was acquitted, the evidence proved that he was intimate with a prominent clergyman who suffered for his connection with Irish rebels.

Armagh and other counties in Ireland were not the only places steeped in disaffection. The spirit of rebellion was universally rampant; but in Ireland the danger was more serious, because there the majority were of one mind in hostility to the Government, and the minority were divided, some having thrown in their lot with the turbulent, while others were in quest of an organisation that would afford them the means of self defence. No doubt the conflicts between the Defenders and the Peep of Day Boys had become intolerable in the County of Armagh, and loyal men could endure them no longer. There were no Peep of Day Boys in the province of Connaught, to which so many Roman Catholics were said to have been banished; yet Connaught was more disturbed than the worst districts in Armagh.

A high authority stated at the time that, "in no part of the kingdom had the disturbances become as formidable, either for the number, the steadiness, or the objects of the insurgents, as in Connaught". There the Defenders, encouraged and actively supported by the exiles from Armagh, had a freehand, and they made the most of it. They levied war against the King; openly marched to give battle to his Majesty's forces, with the professed intention of overturning the Government; took the town of Drumsna by storm; compelled the men employed in the Arigna iron works to make weapons of various kinds for their use; disarmed Athlone; established courts-martial; and adjudged severe punishment to those who dared to appeal to the local magistrates, in some cases three hundred lashes being inflicted.

No one could defend all that had been done by the Peep of Day Boys. The most that the public had to say in their favour was that they were a necessary evil, holding the Defenders in check till more effectual restraints were provided. If they had not met force with force loyal citizens might have had to contend against greater difficulties. This is not written to excuse the lawless actions of the faction. They were a terror to the Defenders, whose violence in Connaught shows what would have happened in Armagh, but for the restrictive influence exercised by people who dogged the movements of those who were in very deed "a lawless banditti", and brought upon themselves the punishment that attracted the pity of Lord Gosford and some of the magistrates of the County of Armagh.

Touching the Speech, and the terms of reproach that base minded writers have endeavoured to fix on the Orangemen, the plainest truths of history have been perverted to accomplish the ungracious object. The calumniators have to stifle historical records in order to gratify their malignity. Eleven months before the Speech attributed to Lord Gosford was delivered, the Irish Parliament was opened by Earl Camden, and pointed reference was made in the Speech from the Throne to the unhappy state of affairs in Armagh and other parts of Ireland. "It is with regret," said his Excellency, "that I feel myself obliged to advert to those secret and treasonable associations, the dangerous extent and malignity of which have, in some degree, been disclosed on several trials, and to the disturbances which have taken place in some parts of the kingdom. It has, at the same time, been a source of great satisfaction to me to observe the successful and meritorious exertions of the magistrates in several parts of the kingdom."

These words were uttered on the 21st of January, 1795, eight months before the Battle of the Diamond, so that the Orangemen, who had no existence as Orangemen, could not be brought within the scope of Lord Camden's observations. Furthermore, on the first day of the Session the Attorney General gave notice that he would introduce a Bill to indemnify magistrates and others who had not conformed to law in their treatment of Defenders, and another Bill to make it a capitol felony to enter into a conspiracy to assassinate. When the Indemnity Bill was presented to the House, Mr. Grattan wished to know more about the violations of the law that were to be condoned. In addition, he demanded the attendance of two of the Judges. The motion was rejected; But Mr. Stanley, who had gone on circuit as an Assistant Judge through many of the disturbed counties, gave the hon. member information on the subject. His opinion may be repeated:

> "He could answer for it that no man who had observed the systematic conduct of the Defenders, their uniformity of principle, and steadiness of pursuit, could doubt for a moment that they acted in concert, and were connected with, those treasonable associations, whose councils ultimately broke forth in an attack on the person of the Sovereign."(*)

These facts indicate plainly enough that the Orangemen were not to be found among the "lawless banditti".

Those who have endeavoured to link the Orangemen to the "lawless banditti" must be content to stand before the world as reckless perverters of history, wearing the penitential garb of wilful or ignorant offenders. `In the first place, the outcry against the Orangemen vanishes in vapour when it is remembered that the outrages alluded to occurred in the Spring season of 1795, months before the Battle of the Diamond, and the meeting held in Sloan's to consider what form and name the contemplated defensive association should assume. This single fact is sufficient to put to shame the maligners of Orangeism. And it does not stand alone.

Here we may inquire more minutely in regard to the authorship of the Speech attributed to Lord Gosford; and at the outset it may safely be affirmed that the noble Lord neither wrote nor spoke the words circulated. The style is too hysterical to have been used by a staid nobleman; the sentences are not what would be expected from the Governor of a County, whose inhabitants were sharply divided by religion and politics. Lord Gosford was a high minded nobleman, a prominent member of the Whig party; but he knew well that among the magistrates were many pronounced Tories, who kept constant watch upon his demeanour as the head of the Executive of the County. These and other considerations tended to make

(*) *The reference is to an attack made upon the King when he was proceeding to open the English Parliament. On his return his Majesty was hissed by a mob. After he left the Royal carriage, it was damaged by stones and mud, and one of the servants was knocked down and beaten.*

him the more careful to rule impartially. Besides, his Lordship was an educated gentleman, and it is hard to believe that he would reduce history to burlesque in order to gratify personal feelings, or to promote the interests of a faction.

It is impossible to suppress indignation when people read of "horrors", many of which were self inflicted, of "persecution" unparalleled, and of other grave charges of the same nature. When the author of the forged document, for a forgery it was, appealed to history, and declared himself unable to find anything like what was going on in a limited district of the County of Armagh, he could not have read, or if he read he could not have remembered, the narrative of 1641, and the ghastly "horrors" which darkened and disgraced that period. In the early years of the current century, when all the circumstances were fresh in the memory of old men of the locality, the prevailing opinion assigned the authorship of the document to the Rev. William Bisset, who was getting a church built in Loughgall, and was much annoyed that operations had to be discontinued, the subscriptions having ceased owing to the turbulent state of the neighbourhood. It has been said that the public instinct is generally a safe guide in such matters; but, as in the case of Lord Gosford, it is not easy to believe that a clergyman would allow a fit of temper to make himself ludicrous.

Rightly or wrongly, The Speech was never generally received as authentic, or as having been uttered by Lord Gosford. The picture was too gloomy to be genuine; the statements were unduly exaggerated; and it is evident the whole thing was the subject of controversy from the beginning. Lord Gosford's son and successor was examined before the Select Committee on Orange Lodges; but his evidence was founded on hearsay; for at the date of the "persecution" he was a very young student in Oxford. With respect to the purport of the Resolutions adopted at the meeting in Armagh, he said, in reply to Mr. William Patten, he thought they "alluded to parties of Protestants banded together, but under the form of Orangemen I cannot say." And, in relation to the Speech, his Lordship said, "I never heard any part of it called in question as to its contents or as to its truth. I have heard it objected to by many persons who disapproved of it." That "many persons" had good reason to disapprove of the document may be inferred from the evidence tendered to the Select Committee by Mr. James Christie.

This witness described himself as a member of the Society of Friends, living on his own property, about two miles and three quarters from the borders of the County of Armagh, where he had resided since the year 1793. In other words, his testimony was second hand. According to Mr. Christie, the outrages originated in 1794, but increased in virulence in the Spring of 1795, extending over nearly all the northern counties. Mr. Christie appears to have studied the various aspects of outrage, and could distinguish between "wrecking", "burning", and "total destruction " of house property. Some of the "persecuted" people were weavers, probably working at low wages, and reducing the value of labour, which stirred up the animosity of the weavers arrayed as Peep of Day Boys; some had life-leases on their cabins and bits of land; but the vast majority were tenants at will, mere squatters.

In the document attributed to Lord Gosford, it was stated that "more than half the inhabitants of a populous County had been deprived at one blow of the means as well as of the fruits of their industry", and driven out of their homes. The population of the County at the date concerned was estimated at more than 130,000, so that we are asked to believe that some 65,000 were plundered and banished! In this connection what had the Quaker to say? He was asked by the Chairman of the Committee if he could form any conjecture of the number of families that had been driven from their homes? Here is his reply:-

> "I cannot form any just idea of it, to ascertain it with certainty; but it was said that several hundreds were driven out of the County, and there must have been, from the number of houses that were destroyed, particularly in the County of Armagh; it was worst there than in any other part of the North of Ireland."

The witness seems to have included in his answer what had occurred in Armagh, Down, Antrim, Tyrone, and Derry, and he could only hear that "it was said" several hundreds of families had been driven out of five counties! This does not harmonise with the statement that 60,000 or 65,000 had been chased out of the County of Armagh alone. The Quaker was no friend to Orangeism. The tendency of his evidence was hostile to the Orange society, whose bands and banners offended him; nevertheless, he put the Speech out of court. If he had stopped there no one would have found fault with what he heard or what was "said" by others. But he went on to state that the Peep of Day boys "merged into Orangeism", a statement unsupported by fact. he was correct when he informed the Committee that their name "completely subsided" after the formation of Orange lodges.

Their performances were ended when the lodges got into working order, and the Orangemen assumed the responsibility of maintaining the peace of the North. Still, Mr. Christie, relying probably upon "it is said", was libellously incorrect when he informed the Committee that the United Irishmen became Orangemen. It would be impossible to utter a grosser calumny, or one standing at a greater distance from truth. There never was, there could not be, a member of the seditious United Irish Society, or of any other illegal organisation, admitted into the Loyal Orange Society. Here is the proof. In the first authorised Rules and Regulations, which were revised by the Grand Orange Lodge of Ireland, for the use of all Orange Societies, and approved November 20, 1798, the Obligation of an Orange Man is set forth, and this is the oath that was administered to everyone at admission:-

> "I, A.B., do solemnly and sincerely swear, of my own free Will and Accord.... that I was not, am not, nor ever will be, a United Irishman, and I never took the oath of secrecy to that Society."

This put Mr. Christie's "it is said" to shame. As an additional safeguard to the purity of the Orange Society, in the event of a member of an Orange Lodge being raised to official rank, an abridged form of the Oath was taken by the Master, Secretary, and Treasurer, each of whom for himself swore:-

> "That I am not, was not, nor ever will be a United Irishman, and that I never took the Oath of Secrecy to that Society."

Yea more, as further protection against the admission of United Irishmen, the Master and Deputy Master swore at their installation, each for himself:-

> "That neither I, nor any other Person for me will admit any one into the [Orange] Society who.... has been a United Irishman, or has taken their Oath of Secrecy."

And this obligation was maintained in successive revised editions of the Rules and Regulations of the Orange Society. The solemn Oath effectually disposes of Mr. Christie's "it is said", and of an opinion that prevailed among a class of people who had no special sympathy with Orangeism. The publication of the Oath at this stage anticipates to some extent the reference that shall be made to the authorised Rules, etc., but it is important as we proceed to, nail every spurious coin to the counter, and destroy the "it is said" slanders of the enemies of Orangeism. Viewed in the light of truth, Mr. Christie's evidence tells for Orangeism. He reduced the number of Roman Catholics expelled from thousands to hundreds; even Mr. Plowden could only discover 5,000 or 7,000 exiles, of whom the people of Connaught soon tired, and would have rejoiced to get rid of them and their turbulence.

But perhaps the most convincing proof that the Speech attributed to Lord Gosford was a forgery is supplied by a communication from Mr. James Verner, of Churchill, who rendered such valuable services in keeping the Defenders of Tyrone on their own side of the Blackwater. The letter was published by Colonel Sir William Verner, Bart., in a small tract intended for private circulation only, and no apology is needed for repeating the portion alluding to the Speech. It is dated 9th of March, 1807, and states:-

> "On my return from Dublin I was informed with your letter of the 3rd inst. As I do not recollect to have attended more than two meetings of the magistrates at Armagh in '95 and '96, at which Lord Gosford was present, I cannot give you any detailed account of those various proceedings, or the application made, which induced Lord Gosford to publish a "handbill" which was circulated over the kingdom, and left gratis at the homes of several of the inhabitants of Dublin. I cannot say that I ever heard of any "famous speech" made by his lordship at any of those meetings. Shortly after [the Battle of the Diamond], I attended a meeting of magistrates in Armagh. I there stated that I was sure, from my own knowledge, and from the information I received, there was a deep conspiracy hatching; yet, with the exception of Mr. Richardson of Richill, and a few more, none of them seemed to believe me. I left the meeting in disgust, and only attended one more.., I was, and am, convinced that Lord Gosford was imposed upon."

This settles the question. Mr. Verner was in the meeting when the Speech was alleged to have been delivered, and he had the use of his ears, but he heard no Speech. The whole thing was a forgery, concocted by people who were in sympathy with those who raised such an outcry against being "persecuted by the Protestants, and that justice was not to be had from the magistrates." The "justice" the Roman Catholics demanded was the right to violate the law with impunity; and not having been permitted to do so, several of them left the County, and went to Connaught. Yea more, Mr. Verner, a man of honour and an upright magistrate, says, "Many persons availed themselves of the opportunity to break their windows and destroy some articles of furniture, in order to obtain, by presentment, compensation at the assizes." They were caught in the act of setting fire to their beds and throwing their bits of furniture into the street; but no one deemed it worth his while to prosecute them as they were quitting the County. Besides, no complaints were made to the committee of Magistrates sitting week after week in the precincts of Armagh Cathedral. The chief wreckers were the Roman Catholics themselves, and they were glad to escape the punishment their misdeeds had incurred. It was a happy deliverance from paying debts to the small shopkeepers and rents to the landlords.

Protestant Associations

When the excitement caused by the "persecution" had partially subsided, another attempt was made to unite the Protestants for defensive purposes. The Mixed Associations had failed, because the Roman Catholics would not join, and the Protestants refused to co-operate with them. These difficulties were obviated by establishing exclusively Protestant Associations. Among the first to move in this direction were the tenantry of the Blacker estate near Portadown. On the last day of February, 1796, they held a meeting, Dean Blacker presiding, and in the forefront of the resolutions was one tendering sympathy to the few Roman Catholics who had holdings on the property, and whose houses had been recently plundered by some Peep of Day Boys.

The Protestants on the estate were an overwhelming majority, and had nothing to fear from their Roman Catholic neighbours; yet they afforded their practical proof of friendship. They resolved to inquire into all circumstances of the outrages; to estimate the value of the damage that had been done; and to reimburse every peaceable sufferer, the fund to be provided by an acreable applotment. It is seldom we meet with such acts of generosity; and in this case the evidence of friendly feeling is the more remarkable as many of the tenants had been in the Diamond Hill camp, a fact showing that the Protestants who took part in the Battle bore no ill-feeling to inoffensive Roman Catholics, but fought in defence of their homes and families. In another resolution it was stated the disturbed conditions of the country called upon every honest man to protect himself and his neighbours. Then all present pledged themselves to do all they could to prevent illegal meetings, and to give information to the nearest magistrate against every person found violating the peace, "be his profession what it may."

The example set by the tenantry on the Blacker estate was generally followed throughout Ulster. Meetings were held in Lurgan, Richill, and various other parts of the County of Armagh, and resolutions were adopted similar to those that found favour with the Blacker tenantry. The same course was pursued in the counties of Down, Tyrone, Londonderry, Antrim, Fermanagh, Monaghan, Cavan, and Donegall. The Grand Juries alas assumed a peace preserving attitude, and their resolutions encouraged the defensive movement.

In Hillsborough, then the rendezvous of the nobility and gentry of the North, an important meeting, over which the Marquis of Downshire presided, was held, resolutions were passed declaring attachment to the King and Constitution, pledging those present to maintain the peace, support the magistracy, and protect the life and property of every individual. Further, the nobility and clergy of Down announced that they were ready to arm themselves, when required by the King, to oppose any and every treasonable attempt that might be made by foreign or domestic enemies.

Those meetings produced beneficial effects for a time. They landlords and tenants together, and secured the help of the clergy and professional classes. In the history of the period we pause to admire the names of the great and high born, whose patriotic instincts were excited - the Marquis of Downshire, the Marquis of Londonderry, Bishops and other dignitaries of the Established Church, parochial clergy, Sheriffs, grand jurors, country gentlemen, lawyers, doctors, all the best of the population anxious to display their loyalty. Archdalls, Atkinsons, Blackers, Blackwoods, Brownlows, Ffordes, Gordons, Halls, Hamiltons, Johnstons, Kerrs, Maginnesses, Maxwells, Obins, O'Neills, Prices, Reillys, Savages, Warings, Watsons, etc., names to conjure with, and having a lien on the gratitude of loyal men.

There was however, nothing permanent in the Protestant Associations, or District Defensive Associations, as they were sometimes called; but good came out of them, although the tenure of their existence was not much longer than that of the Mixed Associations. They taught the Loyalists how to unite; prepared the ground for the Orange seeds that were being sown secretly and publicly; led to the formation of Volunteer Associations in many localities; and stimulated the enrolment of the yeomen. This valuable military force originated in 1796; and it is only fair to officers and men to quote the reference made to them in the Report of Lord Castlereagh's Secret Committee:-

> "Your committee have to observe with great satisfaction, that the estimate for the yeomanry as first laid before Parliament was for a number not exceeding 20,000 men - that in the course of six months above 37,000 were arrayed; and that the zeal of the country had so risen with its difficulties that, during the late rebellion, the yeomanry force exceeded 50,000 men, and might have been encreased to a much greater extent. It is unnecessary to recall to the recollection and gratitude of parliament and of the country the services they have performed during the unhappy struggle in which we have been engaged, sharing all the hardships and dangers, and performing all the duties, in common with the King's regular and militia forces."

They took well to Orangeism, and helped to propagate its loyal principles. One illustration of the connection may be supplied. It is that of Moira Yeomanry Loyal Orange Lodge No. 554. Originally, the Lodge belonged to the yeoman of Moira, County of Down, and is kept up till this date by their descendants. There are several cases of the same kind; but none in which the succession of title and doctrine is more conspicuous. In numerous instances the master and members of an Orange Lodge suffered no change except being dressed in the King's uniform. As Orangemen 30,000 of them were reviewed by General Lake in Lurgan demesne, and complimented for their military appearance.

They were required to take the Oath of Allegiance at enrolment; when invasion was apprehended they were to do duty instead of the regular and militia forces, who were to be withdrawn from their cantonments. In Major General Goldie's communication to Captain Atkinson of Crow Hill, his corps and that of Portadown were ordered to defend the pass between that town and Lough Neagh. The order was dated June 10, 1798. In a circular from Lord Castlereagh, Dublin Castle, 24th August, 1798, it was stated that yeomen disabled in actual service were to obtain the benefit of the Royal Hospital in Kilmainham, according to an Act of Parliament. They were also entitled to receive the King's Bounty.

The infantry did patrol duty in towns, and the cavalry in the country districts. In a general Order of Lord Cornwallis, dated Head Quarters Camp, near St. Johnston, September 9, 1798, after the defeat of the rebels at Castlebar, his Lordship says, "the corps of yeomanry in the whole country through which the army has passed have rendered the greatest service, and, are peculiarly entitled to the acknowledgement of the Lord Lieutenant, from their not having tarnished that courage and loyalty, which they displayed in the cause of their King and country, by any acts of wanton cruelty towards their deluded fellow subjects."

Hence, when the rebellion was stamped out these loyal and independent citizen soldiers were included in the vote of thanks passed in the Irish Parliament to the military forces of the Crown. Indeed, taking all the circumstances into account, the yeomanry may be described as the saviours of Ireland when her state was bad as bad could be. The nation has cause to regret their disappearance at the bidding of legislative "progress", which has not provided a suitable substitute.

Earlier Struggles

The struggle of Orangeism to get into life may well be called a creeping process. many of the earlier initiations were performed behind hedges or in dry ditches, which originated the nicknames "hedgers" and "ditchers". They had still more formidable obstacles to surmount in the declared antagonism of some of the gentry, and the half hearted sympathy of others. As a rule the tendency was to conciliate the enemy, and to sacrifice at the altar of Expediency, even to the extent of victimising a Loyalist occasionally. But Sloan and his friends pursued their own course.

The failure of the Mixed Associations convinced them of the folly of endeavouring to work with the Roman Catholics; and they resolved to make their organisation exclusively Protestant.

This resolution was not formed in hostility to Roman Catholics, to whom the Orangemen never did, and never could, bear animosity on account of their religious belief. Their attitude in this respect was well expressed by Ryan's dinner song, "We hate them as masters, we love them as men." The miscarriage of the Protestant Associations was ascribed to a different cause. It was thought that the landlords, as a class, had not manifested friendly interest in the welfare of the Protestant tenants; and, with a few praiseworthy exceptions, they had taken no part in relation to the Battle of the Diamond and other events of the period.

Among the upper classes generally Whig doctrines prevailed; while the farmers and the linen manufacturers were pronounced Conservatives. Therefore, the humble men, who did not aspire to represent pocket boroughs in the Irish House of Commons, and never expected to be in the employment of the State, decided to have a system of their own creation, and to control it themselves. They wanted something that would stand alone, independent of the short lived whims of political parties, and acting as a magnet sufficiently powerful to attract the loyal elements in every Protestant community.

The Dyan men were all, or nearly all, Presbyterians; the Loughgall men were all, or nearly all, Episcopalians; they had fought together, and they determined to cling together. All things considered, the grandest feature of the Orange Society is the catholicity of its constitution. It is purely Protestant; but not sectarian. From the beginning the door were thrown wide open to members of all evangelical denominations, and indeed of all political parties whose aspirations were constitutional.

The farmers and linen manufacturers to whom we owe the Orange Society were God fearing men; they were familiar with only one Book, the Bible; their combination was not designed to injure any man; what they required was peace to carry on their industries, with security for life and property. These rights they obtained through the influence of the Society they brought forth, and whose first lullaby they sung.

The hopes of the founders were soon realised, as the Orange system spread rapidly in the North, and found its way into other Irish Provinces, chiefly through the instrumentality of the military forces of the Crown - the cavalry and infantry of the regular army, the militia regiments, the Fencibles raised in England and Wales and Scotland, the yeomanry, and the Orangemen who were assigned to do duty, or volunteered to do duty, with certain corps on specially important occasions. At the outset the Orange combinations took the form of clubs, or coteries as they were sometimes called in the phraseology of the day, these Clubs being described as Orange Societies. Nevertheless, the system in them all was the same, the warrants, rules and regulations, and objects were the same.

All the Societies were loyal and peaceable; the members were actuated by fraternal feeling; and they were individually and collectively solemnly pledged to fealty to the Crown and Constitution - the Constitution founded by William the Third, Prince of Orange.

Early Ritual, A Higher Degree

After having agreed to call their Society, Orange, in compliment to the Prince of immortal memory, the next step was to organise it. As already stated, the founders had no claim to be regarded as educated men; they were well to do, and could live comfortably; but their knowledge was limited to the management of their farms and looms. Seriously puzzled to know how to form signs and passwords, and construct a ritual, they resolved to meet in Portadown, on a certain day, to see what could be done in this direction.

They needed something different from Masonry, and the methods of the Orange Boys did not exactly suit their ideas. Accordingly, when their business in the market was transacted, they were observed going into and out of a house in which a Masonic Lodge held its meetings. It happened that, on the evening previous the Lodge had assembled for business, and some minor emblems were not removed.

Just then, Mr. Templeton(*), one of the three gallant fellows who stormed the Faughart Fort, and ended the Battle of the Diamond, inquired what Wilson, Winter, and the others were about. Wilson was the spokesman, and having heard his reply he invited them into the Masonic room, and then and there satisfactory arrangements were made. As might be expected, there was nothing either refined or attractive in the words and tokens and ceremonial; but the influence of the place and its associations can be discerned in the results.

(*) *I had the narrative from his son many years ago, after I had delivered a tentative lecture on Orangeism in Portadown.*

The Very Rev. Dean Waring(**), a worthy Orangeman, who took a prominent and praiseworthy part in reducing the earlier system to order, has enabled us to form some idea of the rudeness that characterised the earlier system, and of the confusion that prevailed among the Orange Societies before being amalgamated in one Society. He was Rector of Shankill (or Lurgan) in the Barony of O'Neill and East, County of Armagh, but ecclesiastically in the Diocese of Dromore, and was subsequently advanced to the dignity of Dean.

As Shankill then had neither parsonage nor glebe, Mr. Waring resided on his estate in Down; yet he accepted the office of Honorary Secretary of the Grand Orange Lodge of County Armagh, and at the request of the members undertook to arrange the Warrants and adjust other matters which had got into a medley. Mr. Waring's initiation took place in the year 1798; but he knew all about the Battle of the Diamond; and had watched the progress of the Orange Society from the beginning. He was examined before a Committee of the House of Lords in 1825; his evidence was printed and published, and there can be no objection to a portion of it being repeated, especially as it illustrates the earlier system as it came from the hands of its unpretentious authors. Here are some of the questions and answers:-

"What was the object of the Society? - The original object of the Society was the protection of the persons and properties of those who joined in it, that had been most violently assailed in part of the County Armagh, and their object was self protection.

(**) *This family, of the ancient House of Waring of Lancashire, became established in Ireland in the time of James the First, when John Waring settled in County Antrim, and married Mary, daughter of Rev. Mr. Clanconnell, and founded Waringstown, building a mansion for himself and a church for the use of the people of the neighbourhood. His descendants have occupied high and responsible positions in the Church, the army, the profession of law, and the shrievalty. The Rev. Charles Waring rector of Eglish near Armagh, is a well known Orangeman (1897). Colonel Thomas Waring, grandson of the Dean was for many years M.P. for North Down. He is a J.P. of Down, Barrister-at-Law, served as High Sheriff of the County, and was Grand Master of the Orangemen of England at the time of his death , which occurred suddenly 12th August, 1898.*

**The Very Rev. Holt Waring, Rector of Shankill, Lurgan
and Dean of Dromore**

"Can you give the Committee any account of the passwords or signs by which the members of the Orange Society knew each other? - Yes, I believe I can. I believe I recollect nearly all of them.

"Did they undergo any change after the time you first became acquainted with them? - Yes, they did, several.

"Can you give any particular account of the earliest, and their changes from time to time? Yes, I can. I have memoranda with me which will enable me to do so. The scheme and system of the first that was instituted, held reference to the exit of the Children of Israel from Egypt. It was merely intended as a private or mysterious selection of signs or questions by which they should know each other, which became absolutely necessary by certain circumstances which had occurred in the County of Armagh previously; and in order that they should know each other for their future protection, they instituted a sort of Catechism, Question and Answer, Signs by which they might know each other; and the first was a Question - 'From whence came you? - From the House of Bondage. Whither do you go? To the Promised Land. How do you expect to get there? By the Benefit of a Password. Have you that Password? I have. Will you give it me? I will divide it with a Brother!' Then the Password was M-I-G-D-O-L, being the name of a town at which the Israelites first encamped. It was contrived by Persons of the lowest Description, just as a sort of Freemasonry among themselves.

"Have these Catechisms any Meaning understood, as between Orangemen, otherwise than is apparent upon the Face of them? - Not any; nor was anything concealed whatsoever.

"It was in short mere gibberish? - Yes, for the purpose of Recognition; and when these were disclosed, or there was any Apprehension of their being so, they were changed. There was always a Second Sign or Password; a sort of Countersign: In that the words were, 'The great I Am hath sent me unto you.'(*) There

(*) *This is alleged to have been the token agreed upon by Hamilton of Enniskillen, and Walker of Londonderry, when they met at Raphoe in 1688 for the purpose of arranging a mode of recognition between both garrisons.*

were a great many Additions to these; in fact as many, I believe, as five or six. There was one in 1795, which was added to again in 1797; another in 1802; there was another in 1820; another in 1823; and another in 1825.

"Were the words of that Catechism at any time selected from any supposed reference to the relation in which Protestants and Catholics stood to each other in Ireland? - I cannot say that they were; they carried on the same Allegory, and might be so construed, thus far, as being a contest between the people of the true Religion, supposed to be under Persecution from those of a worse Religion, as the Israelites were supposed to be persecuted by the Heathens, and protecting themselves from them; I think it is likely that the Protestants might so refer.

"Considering themselves at the time in a state of persecution? - Yes, and they do so still."

If it were possible to call Dean Waring as a witness in this year of grace, he might say, in relation to the persecution of the Protestants, particularly the Orangemen, "and they do so still". Have not the Orangemen been persecuted and prosecuted by successive Governments, their only offence being that they were too loyal? Have not many of them been arraigned at every Court of Assize in Ulster, and sent thence to prison for having publicly displayed their fealty to Crown and Constitution? In the closing years of last century, and even at the expiration of the first quarter of the present century, they considered themselves persecuted, "and they do so still".

Bearing in mind that Templeton, of Portadown, was a prominent Freemason, that Sloan of Loughgall was the same, that Wilson of the Dyan was an "unwarranted"(*)Freemason, and that the materials for the first Catechism were supplied in the presence of Masonic emblems, we are the better able to understand the evidence tendered to the Committee by the Orange Dean of Dromore.

When further questioned, the Dean explained why purple had been selected as an ornament; and indeed he may be said to have laid bare the

(*) *The statement that Wilson was an "unwarranted" Freemason is disputed by R.M. Sibbett and Rev. John Brown, who maintain that his membership was regular.* (**Editor**)

whole Orange system as it existed in the beginning - to have brought into the light of day the genius of the organisation, rude or refined. We may continue the extracts from the Blue Book:-

"Why was there so great an object in preserving secrecy? - Because there have been the greatest pains possible taken to sow division among them; to prevent their being able to defend themselves.

"About the same time that this originated, or soon after it began, but before it had got to any great extent, United Irishmen were established; and there were great pains taken to draw the Orangemen, or those that were supposed to be so, from their allegiance, to join the United Irishmen, and emissaries from all parts were sent into the country, to induce the people, partly by persuasion, and partly by intimidation, to join that rebellious combination which was at the time meditating treason and insurrection; and for this reason it was absolutely necessary, if possible, to exclude all suspicious persons from the meetings of the Orangemen, and to afford protection, if they could, to those who refused to join the United Irishmen; for every act of intimidation was used, and the fondness of the people for associating together, their attachment for Freemasonry, and all those private Associations, gave a particular zest to this mode of keeping them true to their allegiance: for that reason it was countenanced."

This satisfactorily accounts for the exclusively Protestant character of the Orange Society, its signs and passwords, which are more or less found in connection with all religious, all political, and nearly all benevolent organisations. Tests of some kind are required; so that if the Orangemen must be punished for secrecy, it is hard to say who would escape.

The Dean next explained the purport of having Orange and Purple systems, the former being "a sort of noviciate, or probationary state", maintained to secure the purity of the institution, inasmuch as members of the Orange Order had to prove themselves worthy and of good repute before receiving the higher Degree of Purple. The protection of faith and firesides was the chief object of the Orange Society; and that object has been realised. Touching "conditional loyalty", which has been a favourite weapon in the hands of enemies, the Dean's evidence is important:-

"Do you understand your Oath, as an Orangeman, to place you under any other obligation than that under which you before stood as a good subject? - I do conceive it did not make any alterations in the obligations I was under as a good subject and a Christian before.

"The Oath is, 'That I will bear true Allegiance to His Majesty King George the Third, his Heirs and Successors, as long as he or they maintain the Protestant Ascendancy(*) Constitution(**)

What do you mean by the King's maintaining the Protestant Ascendancy? I conceive the Coronation Oath(***) binds the King to maintain the Protestant Constitution in Church and State, and as long as he does so we were bound before, and cannot be more bound now, to pay a true Allegiance to His Majesty; but if we were to suppose that Allegiance is entirely without any reciprocal engagement, the Revolution would, of

(*) *Protestant Ascendancy was, after all, the natural outcome of the Constitution established by William the Third. A brief definition was quoted by Dr. Duigenan in the Irish House of Commons: "A Protestant King of Ireland, a Protestant Parliament, a Protestant Hierarchy, etc.'Protestant electors and Government, the benches of Justice, the army and the revenue through all their branches and details Protestant, and this system supported by a connection with the Protestant Realm of Great Britain".*

(**) *This is not the Oath that was taken by Orangemen. It appears in the Rules and Regulations revised in 1820, and printed and published same year by Alderman Abraham Bradley King - subsequently Baronet - Deputy Grand Master. There is nothing said about maintaining the Protestant Ascendancy.*

(***) *The Coronation Oath was settled by the 1st William and Mary, chapter 6. The portion referred to by Dean Waring is: "Archbishop or Bishop - will you to the utmost of your power maintain the Laws of God, the true profession of the Gospel, and the Protestant Reformed Religion established by Law; and will you preserve unto the bishops and clergy of this Realm and to the Churches committed to their charge all such rights and privileges as by law do or shall appertain unto them or any of them? King and Queen - All this I promise to do.*

course, have been a Rebellion, which we consider to have been the groundwork of the English and Irish Liberty and Safety, and that we are bound to support it as far as our influence can go. Further on, the Dean said, "I feel myself bound in allegiance to his Majesty and the Government, let them make what Laws they may; by the Government I mean the Legislature." He felt himself bound, as every Orangeman feels bound to "Loyalty unconditionally".

"By your Oath as an Orangeman, did you consider yourself as Affixing any new condition to your Oath of Allegiance? - Not any.

"Will you explain, then, with what view the words of the Oath of the Orangeman stand thus: 'I will to the utmost of my power bear true Allegiance to his Majesty King George the Third, his Heirs and Successors, as long as he or they maintain the Protestant Ascendancy, the Laws and Constitution of this Kingdom.' - These oaths and the forms originally instituted by the framers of the Orange Association, were made by persons in very low life, and who, I believe, meant in the doing so to enforce the Original Oath of Allegiance as taken by the people, and the Coronation Oath taken by his Majesty, as established at the Revolution; and their object was, if possible, by any influence of theirs to keep the present Constitution as far from being altered in any way as they could.

"When you state that their object was to prevent the present Constitution, as far as possible, from being in any way altered, do you mean to say altered by Violence, or altered by an Act of the Legislature? - By Violence certainly.

"But not if altered by an Act of Legislature? - No; we acknowledge the Laws, and are bound to support them."

Here we have the true meaning of the Orange Oath. There was absolutely no conditional loyalty involved; no intention to dictate to King or Parliament; no menace against the Estates of the Realm; no design to overawe or limit the functions of the Legislature. The sole purpose, the single object, of the Orangeman's Oath at any time, and in every time, no matter what form it assumed, was, and is, and ever shall be, to protect the

Constitution from being altered by violence. It bound, and binds, the Orangemen to "Loyalty unconditionally". It is, and always was, the shibboleth of loyal men - their earnest, solemn, unequivocal reply to the oaths of Defenders, United Irishmen, and all other seditious conspirators, who pledged themselves to dethrone the King, wreck the Constitution, and extirpate Protestantism; and to do these things by violence, for which traitorous purposes foreign enemies were asked to contribute arms and men and money.

The Orangeman's Oath was framed in harmony with Constitutional standards. The Act of 1689 declared the rights and liberties of the subject, and settled the Succession to the Crown. It excluded those who held "Communion with the See or Church of Rome, or shall profess the Popish Religion, or shall marry a Papist"; and, as a matter of fact, many Royal Families were passed over, notwithstanding their strong claims of affinity, to reach the Electress of Hanover. Yea more, it was enacted by the 13th and 14th of William the Third c.2, sec.2, that every Sovereign of England should at his or her Coronation "make, subscribe, and audibly repeat" a Declaration against Transubstantiation, against "the Invocation or Adoration of the Virgin Mary or any other Saint, and the Sacrifice of the Mass". And to strength Protestant Ascendancy, to make still more secure the Protestant character of the Constitution, it was enacted by the 4th of William and Mary, c.2. renewing the expired 13th of Charles the Second, passed by the Irish Parliament, that all Protestants who settled in Ireland, and wished to be naturalised should take the following Oath:-

> "I, A.B., do sincerely promise and swear that I will be faithful and bear true allegiance to their Majesties King William and Queen Mary. So help me God."

Taking all these things into account, what becomes of the clamour against the Orangeman's Oath? Wherein does it differ from the Coronation Oath? Is not Protestant Ascendancy the cardinal virtue of both? Are not the obligations of the Crown and of the Orangemen identical? The only distinction that can be made between the Protestant in the Orange Lodge and the Protestant who settled in Ireland more than two centuries ago is, that in the one case the oath is voluntary, while in the other it was compulsory. There is nothing in the Orangeman's Oath to excite alarm. It is, in fact, a concentrated expression of the spirit and letter of the Constitution established by the Prince of Orange.

First Warrants

In the beginning the Orange Society or Clubs were imperfectly organised. Each County exercised jurisdiction within itself; and to this fact may be attributed the existence of County Grand Lodges. The Orange authorities have always been cautious when dealing with the old pivots of the institution; and, as far as possible, they avoided change, except when it became necessary in the interest of progress and good government. When a man came to Loughgall in quest of a Warrant to be "worked" in the County of Armagh, or in any other County, he had to produce the highest references, and if these were found acceptable, the next step was initiation. In no case was a Warrant issued until the applicant underwent the ordeal in which he acquired a knowledge of the mysteries of the system. Even then he had to wait for his turn, which sometimes involved staying in Loughgall for many days and nights, often a whole week.

As an illustration of the difficulties that beset visitors to Loughgall, the case of Mr. John Emmerson may be mentioned. He had friends in the County of Armagh, by whom he was introduced to James Sloan as being worthy of initiation. Mr. Emmerson was accompanied by a neighbour, Mr. John Johnston, of Annaghone. They succeeded in obtaining No. 173, commonly called the Rosslea Warrant, which the late Imperial Grand Master - William Willoughby Cole, fourth Earl of Enniskillen - described as the oldest Orange Warrant in Fermanagh. The visit was made early in the year 1796. After receiving No. 173, they craved a second Warrant, which was promised to them, and next morning the application was renewed, but No. 184 (should read 174 - **Editor**)had been issued. Naturally, the Fermanagh men thought they would bring home with them two consecutive Numbers; but, instead of 174, they received 184, the intervening Numbers having gone to other applicants in the meantime.

The Rosslea Warrant(*) was installed in Mr. John Johnston's father's

(*) *The Rosslea Warrant is now (1899) in good working order in Newtownbutler District, and on the roll of members is the name of Robert Johnston, son of Mr. T Johnston and an office bearer for more than half a century. Concerning 184, the history is not less remarkable. At the death of its first Master, the Warrant passed into the hands of his nephew, Mr. Robert Clendining, to whom a renewal was granted on the 15th of September, 1828, signed by Ernest, Grand Master; Enniskillen Deputy Grand Master; Henry Maxwell M.P., Grand Secretary; J. Patterson,*

house in Annaghone, where the meetings of the members were occasionally held; for, when Orangeism was started in the district there was no stated place for the Lodge to sit. Sometimes the brethren assembled in Johnston's, and at other times on a bog bank in the neighbourhood, or at an unfrequented spot, to avoid the interruptions of the disaffected, and the unfriendly criticism of those from whom better might have been expected. Perhaps the most interesting, though not the oldest, Warrant in Fermanagh is No. 315. The Lodge meetings were held in the house of Mr. David Beatty of Lisbellaw, and in it were many of the gentry of that part of the County. It was brought into the County early in 1797, by Mr. Samuel Johnston, a substantial farmer in the townland of Kilsallagh. He was the first Master, and David Beatty was the first treasurer. We shall hear more about it when we come to deal with affairs in 1798. Meanwhile, brief references may be made to two numbers brought into, and still working, in Pettigo district. According to a statement made at the annual meeting October 21, 1898 of the District Lodge, it seems that for years previously the isolated Protestants of Pettigo suffered from the attacks of the Donegal Ribbonnmen, and disorder little short of anarchy prevailed. The turbulence became worse when the United Irishmen's organisation spread over the country. There was no combination among the Protestants of the town, which is partly in Fermanagh and partly in Donegal; but one or other of which parts must be traversed to reach what is known as Patrick's purgatory in one of the Lough Derg islands(*). The introduction of Orangeism, however, met the

---

Deputy Grand Secretary; Henry Brooks, Grand Treasurer; William B. Ward, Deputy Grand Treasurer; countersigned by Enniskillen, County Grand Master, and William Darcy Irvine Grand Secretary. Mr. Clendining acted as Worshipful Master till his death in 1871, at which date his son Mr. Robert Hamilton Clendining was appointed Master, and held the office till 1886, when he removed to another part of Fermanagh. His brother Edward was then elected Master; and, in harmony with the phraseology of the Warrant, "performs the requisite" duties of an office held so long and so worthily by the members of one family. The Warrant is regarded as an heirloom, and is carefully preserved.

(*) The ancient name was Lough Finn; but, Saint Patrick happening to be in the locality, he killed a huge snake, which had been devouring the people's crops. The blood of the creature so coloured the water that the name was changed to Lough Derg (the Red Lough). The legend is absurd. Patricius primus was never in the locality; Patricius secundus, a

wants of the Protestants. They sent a deputation to Loughgall; and as a result, two Warrants were issued - Numbers 679 and 680 - which were speedily embodied, others following in due course.

The same year, 1796, a yeomanry corps - the Pettigo Loyal Infantry - was formed; many of the brethren joined; and, whether as yeomen or volunteers, good service was rendered, by all concerned, during the Rebellion. The District is now No. 10 in Fermanagh, and is in a flourishing state, presided over by Mr. George Archdale, whose elected colleagues are Dr. Aiken, Rev. W. Stack, Mr. J.S. Collins, and Mr. James A. Atkin. In the spring of 1796, Mr. Thomas Boyd, then residing in the townland of Killycorran, near Fivemiletown, County of Tyrone, went to Loughgall, got himself initiated, and brought a Warrant home with him. After his return he convened private meetings, instructed many of his neighbours in the mysteries of Orangeism; and, notwithstanding opposition in high quarters, the work was successful. About the same time the system found its way into Antrim, Down, Monaghan, and other counties.

It was specially active in Belfast by reason of the energy of Dr. Atkinson, and in Lisburn and neighbourhood through the zeal of the Rev. Philip Johnston, Vicar of Derriaghy, and the Rev. Dr. Cupples, of Lisburn. Loughgall was the seat of authority. There, Mr. James Sloan acted as Secretary, and his brother-in-law Mr. Wolsey Atkinson, of Portadown, discharged the duties of Treasurer. As we have said, the counties in the beginning managed their own business; and the arrangements in County Antrim attested skilful hands and earnest hearts.

The Antrim Regulations proved useful to the men of the time, and eminently useful when all the Orange Societies were amalgamated in one Society, and a Book of Rules and Regulations was formed for common use and guidance. There are no records to supply information in regard to those who became possessed of the Loughgall Warrants; but the traditions of the older Orangemen have preserved some of the Masters' names; and it may be interesting to repeat them:-

No.1, as stated previously, was secured by James Wilson, of the Dyan, near Caledon, in the County of Tyrone.

Fermanagh man, founded the station. The penitential exercise was originally performed on the largest island in the lake; but the scene was shifted, in consequence of a melancholy accident on July 12, 1795, involving the loss of 70 lives by drowning while going to the place.

61

No.2 was given to Thomas Sinclair, of Derryscollop, County of Armagh. He became a Lieutenant in the Churchill corps of yeomanry, and discharged the duties of an inspector under the Irish Linen Board. He was a substantial farmer and linen manufacturer; took part in the Battle of the Diamond; and held the position of Master of the Lodge till his death.

No.3 passed to Mr. Bartley, of Derryaughill, between the towns of Moy and Blackwatertown, respectively situated in Tyrone and Armagh. He was a master tailor, and as already stated, was so proud of his prize, and so anxious to communicate the news to his neighbours, that he swam across the Blackwater River, always swollen in Winter, in order to take a short cut to his home.

No.4 fell to Mr. Lockhart, of Knocknacloy, in the County of Tyrone; and my informant, who is now dead, sat in the Lodge as a visitor some ten years ago.

No.5 was allotted to Robert Irwin, of Kinnego, in the County of Armagh. My informant was his son James, an old Orangeman, who said his father was initiated behind a ditch.

No.6 went to a resident in Killilea, County of Armagh, but I failed to discover his name.

No.7 was given to Thomas Lecky, of Breagh, in the County of Armagh. He was a man of resolute character; a leader at the Battle of the Diamond; and among the first to undertake dangerous enterprises. It was he that inflicted severe punishment on O'Neill in Loughgall fair. Among the old people in the neighbourhood the tradition is that Lecky arrived at Sloan's house when No.7 was about to be made out for another person. Lecky, however, flourished an immense blackthorn stick he held in his hand, declaring he would disperse the meeting if he did not get the Number. Therefore, it was assigned to him for peace sake. This Lodge, in the beginning, often met in a limekiln.

No.8 passed to Richard Robinson, of Timakeel, and is still in the Portadown District, but not at Timakeel. [Colonel Blacker handed to the Select Committee on Orange Lodges a No.89, Timakeel, issued July 7th, 1796, and signed James Sloan; and it may be that my informant made a mistake in relation to the No., or, for some reason, No.8 was cancelled, and 89 substituted.]

No.9 was issued to a man in the neighbourhood of Portadown, but I have not been able to discover his name.

No.10 became the property of George Templeton, one of the three who stormed Faughart Fort.

No.28 fell to James Sloan. Among the members were Mr. John Hardy, agent to the Cope estate, and his three sons. The Number sank and rose again three or four times, and was called in and lay dormant until James Stothers took it up in lieu of a later Number. It went to Bond Hill, near Cran-na-gael, and thence into Cran-na-gael, and is working well in Loughgall District. One of the original members was Mr. John Bates, of Ardea, whose grandsons live in the locality.

No.35 became the property of George Innis, who kept an inn in Grange O'Neiland, not far from the Diamond.

No.40 was given to Robert Ruddock, whose grandsons are members of No.7

No.85 was given to Henry Spencer, of Causnagh, near Loughgall. He was one of the joint secretaries to the early meetings in Sloan's. The first treasurer was William Preston of Derrycrew, grandfather of the late Sir John Preston, of Belfast.

No.118 was given to Bernard Lamb, formerly of Druminis near Hamilton's Bawn, and subsequently of Castleraw, near the Diamond. He was the other joint secretary to the first meeting in Sloan's. "Diamond Dan" was a member of this Lodge.

This is all that could be ascertained about the distribution of the Loughgall Warrants in the County of Armagh. The first Masters of Lodges, or their brothers or sons, were at the Battle of the Diamond, and they were not forgotten, not even when they had left the County to reside elsewhere. In the case of Fermanagh one example is afforded.

Early Organisation in County Antrim

Here is another in regard to Antrim. At the date concerned there lived in Lisburn a man named James Hart, formerly of Churchill in the County of Armagh. His brothers and brothers-in-law had been in the Battle, and one of them used to boast of getting away with a whole skin, while his "castor hat" was riddled with balls. It appears that on the night of the 21st of September, 1795, he was of the party doing patrol duty, and he placed his hat upon a hedge for the purpose of decoying the Defenders. The ruse had the desired effect; for, next morning the bullets fell in showers upon the inoffensive headgear, which was no longer serviceable to the owner. James Hart was an important man on the Hertford estate; and he thought the best thing he could do for the Protestant tenants - there were few others - was to make them Orangemen. Therefore, he went to Loughgall, was initiated in Sloan's house, and returned to Lisburn with a Warrant.

The system soon acquired popularity in rural and urban districts. The Vicar had organised his own parishioners, in 1793, under the name of Loyalists, and the feeling spread into the adjoining parishes, so that the soil was well prepared for the new seed that Hart had come to scatter.

The Vicar of Derriaghy was such a prominent loyal man that a conspiracy was formed to murder him, and he was wounded in Castle Street, Lisburn, when about to mount his horse to go to his home in Ballymacash. The bullet entered into the fleshy part of his arm, near to the shoulder, and passed along his breast. And this is not all. Years after the assassin failed to accomplish his purpose, the moral character of the Vicar and his action as a Magistrate of the County were virulently assailed by Mr. Plowden.

The pistol affair was followed by a Government Proclamation offering a reward of £300 for the prosecution of the person who fired the shot; and by meetings all over the country, congratulating Mr. Johnston on his providential escape, while a reward of £1,000 was promised from private sources to whoever would prosecute to conviction, within twelve calendar months, the villain who endeavoured to take the Vicar's life.(*)

(*) The attempt was made between eight and nine o'clock at night, on the 8th of October 1796; but the name of the assassin was not divulged, although a resident of Lisburn was strongly suspected, and has since become known. Mr. Johnson had several escapes from assassinations.

64

He had, however, completed his organisation of the Loyalists, with the approval of Earl O'Neill, Governor of the County, and Lord Castlereagh, Private Secretary to the Lord Lieutenant of Ireland. In its scope the combination embraced eleven adjoining parishes - Derriaghy, Lambeg, Lisburn, Magheregal, Ballinderry, Aghalee, Aghagallen, Maghremisk, Glenavy, Camlin,(*) and Tullyrusk. The Loyalists bound themselves to assist the civil magistrate when called upon to maintain constituted Authority and execute the laws against promoters of sedition and disturbances of the peace.(**)

The organisation was, in principle, a forecast of Orangeism; and Mr. Johnston and his men had no difficulty in joining the system brought from Loughgall by Mr. James Hart. Within one year after James Hart's return Lisburn alone contained 14 Orange Lodges; in the other parishes named Orangeism was quite as strong; and peace prevailed when rebellion raised its head at the town of Antrim and at Ballynahinch. The most friendly feeling was shown to Hart and his Orange system by the two worthy clergymen mentioned and by the clergy generally, as well as by Mr. James Watson, of Brookhill; the brothers Coulson, damask manufacturers, of Huguenot descent; and, generally, by the landed proprietors and large employers of labour.

In the neighbourhood of Lisburn is Blaris Moor, which was then a great military camp, and many of the soldiers were initiated. James Hart was specially well received in Belfast as an Orange agent. Among those who heartily welcomed him were worthy citizens, whose names are still revered in the commercial capital of Ulster, although they have all gone over to the majority. They were Dr. Atkinson, of whom more shall be said; Mr. Henry Moore, of Sandy Row; Mr. Edward May, jun.; Major Fox; Captain Ellsmore; Messrs. William Ewart, father of the first baronet, and descended from the Ewarts of Fermanagh, who were conspicuous Inniskilling Men, James Law, Stephen Daniel, James Suffern, and Christopher Hudson. With such a good beginning, Orangeism soon became vigorous in Belfast and throughout the County of Antrim.

(*) Present day Crumlin. (Editor)

(**) When the Government resolved to form the yeomanry corps, the Hertford estate supplied 71 sergeants, 13 trumpeters or drummers, and 1.500 rank and file.

Even in 1796, the Orange Society was strong enough to make conspirators uneasy. In the Northern Star of March 28, it was stated that "for several days past reports were industriously circulated that those miscreants, the Orange Men, meditated an attack upon the town of Belfast, and were determined to destroy the persons and habitations of those in his country who had promoted the Union of Irishmen." There was not a word of truth in the "reports". The "miscreants" were organised to protect themselves, and not to injure the persons and properties of their neighbours.

Before parting with Rev. Philip Johnston and his Loyalists a few words more may be said about them. As already intimated, they maintained peace and good order throughout a large district of country; strangers who settled in the locality tried in vain to seduce them from allegiance principle; they were accused of all kinds of cruelty and crime, but were honourably acquitted after judicial inquiry. When they resolved to abandon their organisation in favour of Orangeism, they carried with them a clean character. The new name they adopted was "The Boyne Society, commonly called Orange Men, of the County of Antrim;" but they did not forget that they formed a branch of the Orange tree, whose roots were in Loughgall; and in this connection they styled their Society "Royal Orange Association, County Antrim District."

There was something more than caprice connected with the word Royal in the title; for the Government had cognition of every step that was publicly taken. As soon as the Association was formed it was placed under the control of the Right Worshipful Doctor William Atkinson, of Belfast, Grand Master; the Rev. Philip Johnston, Grand Chaplain; Brother William Hart, of Lisburn, Grand Secretary; with the following General Committee: Edward Hogg, Esq., 354 Lisburn; Rev. Philip Johnston, 317 Ballymacash; Thomas McCully, 224 Soldierstown; Michael Boomer, 137 Derriaghy; Stephen Daniel, 238 Belfast; James Innes, 152 Lisburn; John Johnston, 244 Lisburn; Thomas Briggs, 121 Maze; William Johnston, 143 Ballinderry; Thomas Shillington, 403 Aghagallon; William Murphy, 146 Magheragal.

The Grand Master presided, and the Grand Secretary was present at Committee meetings. In drawing up the Rules and Regulations, portions of the Loyalists' arrangements were retained, just as portions of these Rules and Regulations were retained in the Rules and Regulations framed in 1798 for the use of all Orange Societies. In fact, the revisers acknowledge the obligations they were under to the formulae of the Royal Orange Association of the County Antrim. The Antrim Rules and Regulations were constructed by men of intellectual capacity; and it is highly probable that, with slight modification to suit local circumstances, they prevailed in Fermanagh, Monaghan, Londonderry, and other counties. The rules in regard to secrecy and administration of the Order were identical; but the general rules were left to the discretion of masters and Officers of counties. If some were rude, others were less rude, and others were the product of cultured minds.

Original Armagh Rules

Touching the County of Armagh, it is to be regretted that the original rules are not forthcoming; and perhaps the reason is, they never reached a printed form. They seem not to have got beyond the manuscript stage. Nevertheless, it is not unreasonable to suppose that their spirit is in the Antrim Rules and Regulations; and, probably, we have their letter in a Lodge Book belonging to No. 670, issued in 1798 to John Hyde, who had been at the Battle of the Diamond, midway between which village and Loughgall the monthly meetings were held. The Book was found, with other relics, in the Lodge chest a few years ago; and the handwriting of the Rules etc., is vastly superior to that displayed in the other entries. The portion alluded to is entitled "Bye Laws and Regulations of the Orange Society meeting in Ballymagerney, in memory of King William the Third, Prince of Orange."

> The **first** rule binds the members to meet every month, and not to depart without leave from the Chair.
>
> The **second** rule prohibits, on pain of expulsion, drunkenness and disorder, "least the harmony of the Meeting should be disturbed".
>
> The **third** rule prescribes that $11/4\frac{1}{2}$d - an old Irish half guinea - shall be paid by the person depositing a Certificate, while the sum of 1/1d was exacted "for the Certificate drawn out".
>
> The **fourth** rule deals with visitors, who were excluded till the business was over.
>
> The **fifth** rule was as follows: "That No Roman Catholic can be admitted in to Our Society by any mains, and our reason for so objecting against them is in memory of the bloody Massacre which they Committed on Our Forefathers."

The **sixth** rule provided for investigating the character of applicants for admission.

By the **seventh** rule each member of the Lodge was bound to "venture life and fortune" to assist the king and his lawful successors "against All his or their Enimises as loing he or the Maintanes the prodestand Religion ".

In the **eighth** rule provision was made for the expulsion of members who broke the Rules and Regulations.

The **ninth** rule may be quoted as it appears in the Lodge Book: "That We are to mete the 12 Day of July in Evrey year and go to Whatseover plase of Worship Shall bee aggred upon and our reason for so meeting and Assembling on that Day is in Memory of King William the prince of ororrnge Who bravly Suported and freed us from Popish Slavery Which ought to bee kept By all true prodestants thrughout his Mayestys Dominon."

The **tenth** and last rule warns all persons not to seek admission, if they think they cannot conform to the Laws and Constitution of the Lodge.

Here we have probably a transcript of the Rules and Regulations as they were originally framed. They were kept in Sloan's house in Loughgall, and every man who took out a Warrant had to make a copy of them for the use of his Lodge. The orthography and syntax are not the best; but much of the blame rests with the copyist, who could spell correctly enough when he chose to do so.

The principles, however, were sound; and to promulgate and maintain them always was, and still is, the prime object of the Orange Society. Moreover, the grammatical defects are not worse than are sometimes found in MSS, of the period, whose authors were more pretentious than the worthy Master and members of the Orange Lodge that met in Ballymagerney. The Book contains general statements as to income and expenditure during eleven years. few particulars are disclosed. There are, however, several entries leading to the belief that, from the beginning, the members had to claim to "benefit". On the 17th of March, 1799, a small sum was allotted "to funeral from the waste lands"; and on three other occasions contributions were paid towards funeral expenses. On the 14th of May, 1800, the sum of 11/5 was voted "to the poor"; and on the 12th of July, 1801, an entry shows that a small amount was spent on "ribbon", no doubt for a procession.

These particulars help us to form an idea of the working of the earlier Orange Lodges. But more important is the information supplied by the Rules. Therein we discern the reason why the Society was called Orange; we can understand the grateful feeling of the Protestants for the deliverance wrought out for them by the victory of William the Third at the Boyne, which was to be commemorated every 12th of July; and we can discover the current of thought that led to the Society being exclusively Protestant. This exclusiveness was not dictated by what had occurred either at the Battle of the Diamond or at the Battle of the Boyne. The fifth rule brings us back to the "Bloody Massacre" in 1641; and old men living in the closing years of the eighteenth century might be excused if they excluded from their Association the descendants of the people who had barbarously treated their "forefathers". Loughgall was the centre of a district that had suffered severely from the effort of the Roman Catholics to utterly extirpate the Protestants of Ireland. The inhabitants of that town needed not to travel from their own homes to see marks of human malice. They heard of the hundreds drowned at Portadown and in other parts of the Bann River(*); of the hundreds who met a like fate in the Blackwater River, in the mill pond of Killyman, in the Toll River, in the lough at their own doors in the demesne of the Lord of the Manor; and every morning they could look at the old church into which the rebel Colonel Dogherty drove three hundred Protestants whom he had stripped of their clothing, and vowed that they should all be put to death.

After four days' imprisonment, with poor allowance of food, and no bedding but straw, the rebels began their bloody work in the church, stabbing, quartering, or otherwise cutting in pieces more than one hundred of the unfortunate prisoners, only desisting when Captain O'Reilly ordered the work of destruction to cease. Next day the survivors, many of them wounded, all of them naked, were turned out of the church to wander through the country, depending on the "cold and sorrowful charity of the usurping, merciless, and pitiless Irish".(**) It was the history of the Bloody Massacre that was present to the minds of the founders of Orangeism when they determined to make their Society exclusively Protestant.

(*) According to the deposition of Thomas Green of Drumcree, 4,000 Protestants were drowned in the County of Armagh.
(**) Examination of Alice Gregg, widow of Richard Gregg, late of Loughgall Harleian MSS. quoted by Miss Hickson.

Problems of Rapid growth

The existence of so many Orange Societies was found to be unsuitable in many ways. In some places the system spread so rapidly that local men could not keep it under proper control; in other places persons who were not altogether worthy got themselves initiated. The Defenders were committing outrages in many counties, and the Protestants whom they had plundered were retaliating. Upon the Orangemen, however, the enemy laboured to fix the blame - the enemy at the time consisted of rabid Roman Catholics and weak kneed Protestants, whose successors do not show much sign of improvement. In addition, the most malicious rumours were circulated to the prejudice of the Orangemen.

Here is a sample in a communication from Rev. Edward Hudson to the Earl of Charlemont(*):-

> "1796, May 29, Portglenone, Ballymena. - 'A few days previous to a fair which was lately held in the town of Antrim, a report was circulated that a number of Orangemen (from the moon I suppose) were to be there in order to fall upon the [Catholics]. However absurd and improbable such reports are, in the present state of things here they have spread a panic amongst that description of people which we who love union have not been able to dispel, though I assure you no pains have been spared for that purpose. The fear of the brethren has induced a change in the ceremony of initiation, which is now performed *"coram unotantum"* " (**Editor** - 'one at a time').

Mr. Hudson had an itch for writing; and it would have been well for his reputation if pen and ink had been put away from him. One time he wrote favourably, and at another time unfavourably, of the Orangemen. Remembering what had occurred at Forkhill, when an assassin fired at him, and the bullet took effect upon the horse he was riding, he must have been deceived by memory to describe himself as one of those "who love union" with Roman Catholics. But he was addressing the Patriot Earl, who testified subsequently that he did not care for this "union". Such vacillation brought trouble to the Protestants of Ireland, and has left them comparatively powerless to-day. It would be a pity to deprive men like the Rev. Edward Hudson of the pleasure to be derived from new friends, behind whose dissimulation the blunderbuss could be seen.

(*) Lord Charlemont had been Commander of the Volunteers 1778-1784.
*(**Editor**)*

First Processions: 12th July 1796

But no slander could interrupt the progress of the Orange Societies. The Orangemen had learned to despise the flattery of pretended friends and the hatred of avowed enemies. Having survived course misrepresentation and courser nicknames, they felt that the time had come to show themselves in public. Accordingly, they resolved to hold their first procession on the 12th of July, 1796.

The Societies were young; but the members were numerous, showing how rapidly the system had spread; and its adaptability to the social and political necessities of loyal citizens. It was a great venture to appear outside the Lodge Rooms; still, there was no mode of escaping the obligation imposed by the Loughgall Rules, the Antrim Rules, and the Rules of every County in Ulster. Therefore, upon the anniversary of the day consecrated to civil and religious liberty the Orangemen turned out. " 'Twas on a Tuesday morning, the sun rose bright and clear." With the exception of the County of Armagh, the parades were small; the style of the regalia had not been settled; some wore ribbons; others had no symbols of any kind; but nearly all carried firearms, as they expected to be assailed. Brief reference to what occurred may be interesting.

Fermanagh and Monaghan

The first "Orange walk" in connection with Fermanagh and Monaghan was promoted by the master and members of No. 184, who arrayed to unite for the occasion with a Lodge held in the Black Kesh, in the County of Monaghan. Both Lodges joined at the village of Killevan, where they were confronted by a Magistrate, who challenged the proceedings, thinking that the object was to create disturbances. The masters of the Lodges halted their men, and conferred with the arbiter of justice. They told him who they were, what were their intentions, and assured him that every individual in the assembly was solemnly sworn to defend Crown and Constitution. When the words of the Orange oath were repeated, the guardian of the peace exclaimed, "Why, our obligations are identical; we might exchange oaths any day; the procession may move on, and I wish the Society success." Yea more, his Worship offered Mr. Johnston £50 for the Warrant; but twice the amount would not have bought it.

Tyrone

On the same day, about fifty of the brethren walked in procession along an old road leading from a place known as Johnston's Chapel to Ballagh in the County of Tyrone. The Warrant for Ballagh Lodge was taken out by Mr. Robert Trimble, whose grandson, Mr. Robert Trimble, succeeded to the office of master. The first display was a stolen march, and it was not the only stolen one in Ulster.

Armagh

In the County of Armagh, however, there was a magnificent demonstration, which pleased and encouraged the Orangemen and their friends, while it excited the ire of opponents, whose name was legion. Here is the report that appeared in the Belfast News Letter of July 15, 1796:-

> "We understand that, on Tuesday last, being the anniversary of the Battle of Aughrim, a great body of Orange Men amounting to upwards of 2,000 assembled in Lurgan, and spent the day with the utmost regularity and good order. It unfortunately happened in the course of the afternoon that some words took place between Mr. McMordie, at Aghalee, near Lurgan, and one of the Queen's County militia, when coming to blows McMordie received a stab of which he died."

There was nothing in the procession to stir up the choler of the militiamen, or of any other man. The only emblems worn by the processionists were Orange cockades, pinned on the right shoulder, on the hat, or on the breast of the coat. Those who were entitled to do so fixed a blue ribbon in the button-hole of coat or vest. Neither sashes nor collars had come into fashion, and such a thing as an orange cloak was not thought of. Each Lodge had its own banner, and the music was supplied by fife and drum, which are still considered orthodox Orange instruments. On one side of the banner was painted an equestrian statue of William the Third crossing the Boyne; and on the other side a picture of George the Third, or of some local favourite. The flag that was borne at the head of one of the Loughgall Lodges deserves special notice.

In 1782, the owner of the Loughgall estate, Lieutenant Colonel Robert Camden Cope, raised a troop of Volunteers, and his daughter made a flag of blue silk, which she embroidered with the Royal Arms, and presented it to the troops. When the Orange Society was instituted, and the brethren resolved to commemorate the Boyne anniversary, the flag was given to "Little" Jemmy Sloan for his Lodge, No. 161, and it was an attractive object in the premier procession in the County of the Diamond. The banner at the head of No.2 - Lieutenant Sinclair's Lodge - was attractive. Immediately the news was circulated about the good fortune of No.161, a special meeting of No.2 was summoned to consider what to be done in relation to having a banner at the head of the procession. At the special meeting several officers from Charlemont Fort were present; and one of them, Major Dalton, contributed five guineas of the sum required.

Hostile Press Reaction

Now we may hear what the enemy had to say about this orderly procession. In the Northern Star of July 15, a report was published; and, perhaps, never before nor since was a grosser calumny circulated. The words are as follows:-

> "On Tuesday last (12th July, or 1st O.S.)(*) the Gentlemen called Orange Boys, who have desolated the County Armagh during the last year, paraded publicly in large bodies, with orange cockades and colours flying, through the towns of Lurgan, Waringstown, Portadown, etc. Their colours, which were new and costly, bore on one side King William on horseback, and (will it be believed?) on the reverse King George the Third!!!! This banditti, who have hunted upwards of 700 families from their homes and their all - who have put the Catholics of the County out of the "King Peace", parade in open day under bearing the King's effigy, and sanctioned by the magistrates!!

(*) For the information of any Orangeman who may not know what the initials mean it may be stated that the ancient modes of determining the length of the year led to grave confusion. Lunar time and solar time could not be reconciled; and some of the Pontiffs played tricks with the question. The Julian calendar was found to be too long, and Gregory XIII took the matter in hand. Finally in 1751 an Act was passed in the English Parliament taking away eleven days, making the year to begin on the 1st of January. Hence the 1st of July became the 12th the day on which the Battle of the Boyne is commemorated and with it the Battle of Aughrim. This is the new style.

Irishmen! Is it not plain enough? One of their captains, of the name of McMordie, was killed in the afternoon in an affray with some of the Queen's County Militia."

This vile calumny did not satisfy the enemy. In the Northern Star of July 18, a writer, under the date "Tandragee, July 13, 1796", says:-

"Happening to be yesterday in Tandragee, I saw with feeling and honest indignation, a grand division or party of Orange or Break-of-day men who, on pretence of celebrating the anniversary of the Battle of the Boyne, were, in reality, celebrating their own disgrace and degradation of their country, or rather were rejoicing for the many ravages, devastations, rapes, and murders committed with unrelenting fury on the defenceless Catholics of this loyal County.

The procession consisted of fourteen companies, each with ensigns and devices emblematical of the occasion, and formed a motley group of Turncoats, Methodists, Seceders, and High churchmen at least double of all the rest, with a multitude of boys and country trolls cheering up the lagging heroes.

The pious Rector of the parish was seen bringing up the rear, conversing delightfully with the most ragamuffin of them, exulting in the happy sight, and praying for their success - as much as to say, 'Go on, my boys, and prosper; fear not, I am with you, glorious defenders of the faith!' The Orange cockade denoted, as I was informed, such as had taken the Orange oath: viz. - to be true to King and Government and to exterminate the Catholics.

The Blue denotes the Freemasons, who, though well-affected to the cause, cannot as yet be induced to break the sacred tie of friendship and brotherly love. The Orange and Blue intermixed are a hardy race, the mongrels of Church and State, who, though Masons, are blind to the sign and badge of Union, refuse the hand of friendship, and think it no crime to plunge the mid-night dagger in the bosom of a brother! How man can thus divest himself of all sense of shame, honour, religion, and humanity, or how such miscreants can be encouraged to show their face in open day, is what I can't explain, unless there be some wonderful dispensing power lately imported to this island, or changing sided with Dr. Woodward's(*) papists, they prove to the world that themselves hold there is no faith to be kept with Catholics. I could not help observing that the Harp was thrown to some neglected corner on their standards, or trod on by a furious great man on horseback; that the name of Liberty Boys was more execrated by the crowd than that of Romans, and that the Green was the most detested of colours. Poor Ireland! said I, as they have left your fields desolated - as they have bartered your honour and freedom for the smile, or rather grin, of some pensioned hireling, so they would strip you of the beauties with which nature has arrayed you. Thank God, in the other counties of Ireland they order things otherwise."

It was a struggle between the editor and the correspondent which of them could throw more slander at the Orangemen; but, while engaged in their ungracious task, both testified to the magnitude of the first Orange procession in the County of Armagh. In number 2,000 at the lowest estimate, they met at Lurgan, sometimes called Little England, Loughgall, Portadown, Tandragee, Waringstown, Lurgan itself, and other places supplying large contingents. This simple fact disposes of the calumnies. And it does not stand alone. Mr. McMordie was not to blame for the dispute with the Queen's County militiamen, by whom he was killed, and who was tried, found guilty, and punished. The fellow's name was James Delaney. A few days after the occurrences, he was arraigned before Mr. Justice Chamberlain, at Carrickfergus Assizes. The case lasted about two hours, and a great deal of evidence was produced on both sides. The jury found a verdict of manslaughter; and the prisoner was sentenced to be burnt in the hand, which was inflicted in the presence of the Court. After all, the punishment was mild, considering the fact that an innocent man's life was taken by a person wearing the King's uniform.

(*) Richard Woodward, Bishop of Cloyne, 1781-1794. He had been Dean of Clogher. An eminent Irishman, Dr, Haliday, of Belfast, writing to Lord Charlemont under date December 4, 1791, had a good word to say for his Lordship: "In support of what he thought truth, Cloyne boldly hazarded a deal of offence and a deal of mischief." He was conscientious in all his works, even when labouring to reclaim the Roman Catholics (see 13th Report Historical Manuscript Commission 1894)

The Protestant jury, however, spared the offender, and justice was sufficiently vindicated. James Delaney was not the only one whose fingers and hand were burned for slandering a loyal organisation. It is said that Hercules had to grapple with the snakes in his cradle; and Orangeism had to battle with snakes and sneaks in its cradle, in its infancy, in its manhood, and throughout its whole career. Nevertheless, it lives and thrives and goes forward. If all the crimes attributed to the Orangemen were carefully investigated the result would be the same as in McMordie's case. Dr. Madden has devoted a chapter to what he calls "Orange atrocities", not one of which can be traced to Orangeism. The outrages were perpetrated by the disaffected, and in every instance the forces of the Crown, not the Orangemen, retaliated on the miscreants.

Take a few examples. In the County of Meath a number of Defenders assembled; a party of soldiers was sent to disperse them; a few of the lawless banditti took refuge in a gentleman's house; the soldiers entered, and killed them. In the County of Louth, the Defenders and a squadron of Dragoons came into contact; the Defenders were cut down, and those who escaped the sword were driven into a river and drowned.

In the County of Cavan, the Defenders appeared in force near the village of Ballanaugh; when the soldiers arrived the enemy fled into the village, and many of them hid under beds; the village was burned.

In the counties of Westmeath, Longford, and Monaghan pitched battle occurred between the army and the Defenders. In Connaught there were combats of this kind; and after each victory the soldiers are accused of committing "atrocities". In the village of Kilrea, County of Derry, the conflict was between the army and the United Irishmen; the village was demolished all but four houses.

In the County of Fermanagh, a party of Essex Fencibles, accompanied by the Enniskillen Yeomen, marched to the house of a man named Potter, within five miles of Enniskillen, and had an order to arrest him on the charge of being an United Irishman; the accused was absent; his house was burned; Mrs. Potter, who boasted of her husband's politics, and her children were turned into the fields.

In the County of Armagh, June 1797(*), a party of the Ancient Briton's proceeded to the house of an innkeeper in Coolavill to search for arms; but, instead of arms, they found a number of countrymen drinking, carrying on their conversation in Irish; the soldiers used their swords, and dispersed the company, a few of whom were "maimed desperately".

In the County of Down, same month and year, a party met at an inn in Newtownards, and it is alleged they were heard uttering seditious words. The innkeeper, a Mr. McCormick, refused to give the names of those who were present, and he was arrested, and his house demolished. In this case, as in others, Dr. Madden has perverted truth, and appears before the public as a huckster of calumny. "Billy" McCormick kept a public house on the site subsequently occupied by a grocery establishment. "Billy's" house was not wrecked by the Orangemen, but by a party of York Fencibles, accompanied by a detachment of yeomanry acting under military orders.

Many years after, when the house was being rebuilt by a man named O'Neill, a puncheon of whiskey was found covered up in the ashpit, probably to evade the eye of the excise officer. Dr. Madden however, has mis-stated the charge against "Billy". It was more serious than refusing to tell who were in the house. The charge was that "Billy" would not give information concerning the purchase of ammunition for the United Irishmen. Two of the men who had been in the house on the occasion were arrested on a similar charge, and were publicly flogged in what is now Conway Square. One of them died from the effects of the punishment. The house of Dr. Jackson was torn down, as he was suspected of being an United Irishman; and for like reason many other houses in that town and barony were demolished by English Fencibles.

(*) In November of this year, Robert Livingston, Coroner for Armagh, wrote to Lord Charlemont, complaining of the action of "Jonathan Seaver, Esq., Captain of the Orior yeomen, with a party of the ancient British or Welsh cavalry, quartered at Newry" they visited the townlands of Granemore and Carclea they were reported to have burned all before them, and to have taken the arms from the Protestants of Carclea. Subsequently they visited Tassagh where the performances were repeated. These doings have been ascribed to the Orangemen, by a recent caricaturist; but Livingston said they were the work of the yeomen; and, viewed in their worst light, they were nothing more than reprisals.

These are only a few examples of the devastation in the unhappy period, when United Irishmen and Defenders were promoting anarchy, and exulting at the arrival of the French fleet in Bantry Bay, which was scattered by the wind in a few days.(*) Doubtless the retaliation of the military was severe; but their ire was excited; soldiers had been houghed in the streets; poisoned on sentry, waylaid, sometimes beaten to death; and revenge might be expected under such circumstances. If there be any blame in this connection, it rests on the troops, and not on the Orangemen.

Dr. Madden sacrificed his literary reputation at the shrine of bigotry. He wrote the "Orange atrocities" chapter on the authority of an anonymous correspondent; but the anonymous writer did not always drag in the Orangemen. Nevertheless, the Doctor, who was accustomed to deal in sensational affairs, piled horror upon horror, and over the ghastly heap wrote "Orange atrocities", although there was nothing Orange connected with them.

The anonymous correspondent did venture to specify two or three outrages in which he said the Orangemen were concerned; but his judgement was led captive by his ignorance. One example may suffice. It is stated that, in January, 1796, "a party of Orangemen, the Peep-Of-Day Boys having assumed this new designation", visited the house of Daniel Corrigan, in the parish of Kilmore, County Armagh, and took away his fire-arms. After leaving the premises they returned and shot Corrigan dead.

Such is the story; and here is the reply: In the first place, Dan had no right to possess fire-arms; in the next place, the Peep-Of-Day Boys never became Orangemen; and, in the third place, the Boys were still operating in their own account. The feuds between them and the Defenders had degenerated into personal enmities. That William Tremble and a band of Peep-of-Days committed the outrage alluded to is not denied. Tremble was tried at Armagh Assizes, on Wednesday, April 6; found guilty; and sentenced to be hanged and dissected on the Saturday following.

There must, however, have been mitigatory circumstances, for the sentence was commuted, and the culprit was sent into the service of the fleet. As

(*) *The British Fleet was commanded by Admiral Sir George Elphinstone, and the land forces by Lieutenant General Dalrymple who described the conduct of the people as "most meritorious".*

regards the Orangemen, the calumny stands self-condemned. The crime was committed about three months after the Battle of the Diamond, at which date there were no Orangemen.

The Society was only in process of formation, and when formed the members were on the side of law and order. Bad as this sample is, one still worse remains. In a book professing to be a History of Orangeism, published a few years ago, a vile slander is circulated. It is to the effect that, on the night of 22nd September, 1795, a party of Orangemen attacked a Priest's house in the neighbourhood of Portadown, while he was "piously engaged in reading his Office". In addition to the Priest, there were in the dwelling his niece and her son and on old woman. One of the "gang", it is alleged, sent a bullet through the window and a man entered; then the remainder rushed in after smashing the door, and made their way upstairs to the rooms in which the three persons were sleeping. The priest was wounded; the boy's eyes were put out; his mother was disgraced and murdered; the servant escaped, but died in her hiding place; the blind boy wandered about a maniac, and was lost sight of in the rebellion of '98, having possibly fallen a victim to the brutal yeomanry of those days. The chapter of horrors ends with the priest being hanged from one of the rafters of his humble cabin, and the cabin was burned. Such is the narrative, and it is related on the authority of an anonymous pamphleteer, who described the burglars and murderers as Orangemen!

The whole story is a gross slander. Upstairs in a humble cabin is very like "up stairs in a tent". Two hours before midnight, at which time the outrage is alleged to have been committed, the priest was reading his Office. The calumny defeats itself, and is, perhaps, the vilest on record. It is not a shadow of truth. At the date named - the 22nd of September, 1795 - the Battle of the Diamond was only ended, and "victory seemed to waver". There was not then an Orangeman in the world. Sloan and his friends had not met in Loughgall to discuss the form their organisation should take, or whether they would have any organisation at all. Besides, when the Orangemen did appear, it was no part of their business to injure Roman Catholic priests. On the contrary, their obligations bound them to assist in protecting all peaceable citizens, let their religious belief be what it might. There is proof positive that in every case requiring their aid these obligations were fulfilled.

The Behaviour of A True Orangeman

Here is one example: In a period of grave trouble in the County of Armagh there lived a respectable farmer named Carroll. He was married, and at the time referred to there was one child, a very young lad. On a certain night Carroll and his wife and their son retired to rest, one bed accommodating the three persons. At the dawn of day next morning their slumber was suddenly interrupted by a man in "birth day costume" bursting open the door, and springing into the bed without further ceremony. Immediately, Mr. and Mrs. Carroll jumped out, the latter almost frightened to death. The stranger, a priest, explained that his house had been attacked by a band of desperadoes, but whether they were Peep-Of-Day Boys, Defenders, or United Irishmen, he could not tell, as he had to run for his life. He knew he had no claim on Mr. Carroll, who was an Orangeman; but he implored his protection, and his prayer was heard. The brave Orangeman seized his gun; the wife armed herself with the bayonet, and half dressed, they took post at the door, while the priest and the lad remained in the bed. A few of the pursuers approached the house; but when they saw the armed Orangeman and his wife they faced about and retreated. Thus the life of the priest was saved. The child grew to man's estate, and became an Independent Minister, well known in Richill and Armagh city, and esteemed by all who knew him. A devout clergyman, he was called to his reward many years ago; and from himself the facts stated were heard by the writer.

And here is another example of Orange friendship to a Roman Catholic priest: On the night of the 12th of June, 1798, all Lisburn was alarmed by a rumour that Harry Munro(*), a rebel leader, and a large body of his men, meditated a descent on the town for the purpose of burning it and killing the inhabitants. Horse and foot soldiers paraded in the streets; and an order

(*) Munro was a native of Lisburn, and had been a Volunteer. In 1795 he joined the United Irishmen, and commanded the insurgents at the Battle of Ballynahinch, 13th of June, 1798. Deserted by those upon whom he had relied, he fled alone to the mountains; was captured, tried by court martial, and executed in Lisburn opposite his own door. When mounting the ladder he handed his watch to Mr. James Hart informing him to whom it was to be given. Orange James Hart was one of the yeomen on guard at the execution. Harry had had more than enough of the United Men.

was issued to have lights extinguished and doors closed at eight o'clock, while due precaution was taken to guard against the threatened invasion.

An Orange Lodge was sitting that night in a house in Market Square; and at a late hour one of the members who had come out of the room to witness the stirring scenes, saw the parish priest making his way homewards. He went to the old gentleman, and on inquiring learned that his reverence had been attending a sick call. "You can hardly go home with safety Mr. Magee," said the Orangeman. "Much excitement prevails in town, and, as you live a mile out, it would be a great risk for you to go alone; come in for a short time, and we shall arrange to escort you home." The priest thanked the Orangeman, and followed him to the lodge room, where he was hospitably received; and after spending some time with the brethren, four of them accompanied him to his residence.(*)

These and other examples to be supplied hereafter, attest the desire of the Orangemen to live on friendly terms with their Roman Catholic neighbours - priests and people. The Orangemen did not disturb the peace, which they were sworn to maintain; and, in relation to having committed outrages, they defy their accusers. Crime and outrage dogged the career of the United Irishmen and the Defenders.

Every impartial newspaper of the period can be produced to support this statement. In 1796 and 1797, the Defenders troubled Leinster, Munster, and Connaught, while in Ulster the United Irishmen harassed every interest, and deprived life and property of all security. They had their head quarters in Belfast, and parts of Antrim, with the whole of Down, were doomed to suffer by their misdeeds. They wrecked and plundered houses, promoted disorder in fairs and markets, and fought against the military in the County of Derry.(**) They had in Belfast their Inner Circle - an Assassination Committee - whose career is tracked in blood, menacing the existence of the social fabric. Here are specimens of the barbarous deeds perpetrated(***)

(*) The late Hugh McCall of Lisburn, afforded a place to this anecdote in his interesting work on the Staple Manufacturers of Ireland. He was not an Orangeman.
(**) Londonderry Journal.
(***) Culled from the pages of the Belfast News Letter, the source of much of the information circulated in McSkimmin's History of Carrickfergus.

On Tuesday, 5th January, 1796, a man was found drowned near the paper mill, Belfast. The body, which had lain in the water all the preceding night, had on it a blue surtout, a blue body coat, black waistcoat, leather breeches, and "cunnemara" stockings. In one of the pockets of the surtout was the weight of a clock. The man's name was Phillips, he was a friar; supposed to be an informer; and the foul deed was ascribed to the Assassination Committee of the United Irishmen. August 7, the body of a man was found in the river near Strandmillis. A Court of Inquiry was held before the Sovereign of Belfast and Mr. Stewart Banks, and a verdict of accidental death was returned.

A paper found on the person of deceased showed that his name was Joseph Conolly, a private in the City of Limerick Militia, and had leave of absence from the regiment for 31 days. It was alleged that he, too, was an informer; and, to divert attention from the Assassination Committee, it was rumoured that his comrades had thrown him into the river. About the same time the body of a soldier, supposed to have been murdered, was cast on the shore near Holywood. On Friday night, August 19, as sergeant Lee, of the Invalid Company quartered at Carrickfergus, was travelling towards the Camp at Blaris he was fired upon. A ball and several slugs were lodged in his body. Some of the suspected were prosecuted, but acquitted.

On the evening of the 19th of October a man named William McBride, who had lately arrived from Glasgow, was shot dead near the head of North Street, Belfast. He was reported to have been an informer. A few evenings after, a man was shot dead near the County of Down end of the Long Bridge , Belfast, and his body was thrown into the river. October 29th, the Rev. John Cleland was fired at while passing along the streets of Newtownards. On the 31st of the same month, a man named Stephenson, servant to Mr. Gurdy, near Newtownards, was murdered at his master's door, and in his last depositions he named the murderer. About the same time, John Kingsbury, of Belfast, an Orangeman, was murdered near Drum Bridge. He had uttered some words against the United Irishmen.

The records for 1797 are quite as bad. Mr. Cunningham, one of the Newtownards cavalry, was murdered in his own house, and his firearms carried off. An informer named McClure was murdered near Ballymena. A man supposed to have been an informer, was shot near Dunadry. Another supposed informer, named McDowell, was shot at his own door near Dromore. Another suspected informer, named Morgan, was shot in the vicinity of Downpatrick by persons who came on horseback from Ballynahinch. Neal McKimmon, a soldier, of the Argyle Fencibles, was murdered between Lisburn and Blaris camp. The house of a man named McCluskey, County of Derry, was burned, and he was murdered. A man was murdered near Magilligan, same County, because he said he had seen men exercising at night. In same County a man named Lenegan, had his ears cut off and his property destroyed. Richard Harper, of Saintfield, County of Down, alleged to be an informer, was murdered on his way to Belfast; the place was thenceforward called Harper's Bridge.

These are a few examples of the deeds of the Assassination Committee of the United Irishmen and their sympathisers in Ulster. There was not even the shadow of liberty in the province. Life was taken on suspicion; whispers were punished with death; property was ruthlessly destroyed; and the very framework of society was menaced. Yet, little is heard about such doings; while the crimes unfairly imputed to Orangemen are magnified into rank blasphemy against the State. The disorder in Ulster, not to say anything in regard to the other provinces, torn asunder as they were by outrages of every kind, may be referred to as showing the necessity that existed for the Orange Institution to protect life and property, and check the march of redhanded anarchy.

The Orange Society Encouraged by Governments

There is abundant evidence to prove that, when the Orange Society was in process of formation, and after having been formed and organised, it received direct encouragement and support from the Government. On this point, Colonel Blacker's testimony(*) is invaluable, and it may be quoted, bearing in mind that the first attempts to hold processions were made in 1796:

> "Did you ever hear or know of processions being countenanced by the Government?
> Certainly I did.
> "Upon what occasion in particular?
> I remember the military authorities of the northern districts reviewing the Orangemen very regularly.

(*) Select Committee on Irish Lodges, 1st August 1835 (Mr. John Wilson Patten in the chair.)

"Will you state the period and the names of the officers who so reviewed them?

It was in the year 1797, in the town of Lurgan; General Lake was the commander - in - Chief of the northern district; he was there with a full staff, and I think general Knox was there, who was in high command in that district.

"Were you yourself present?

I was.

"What would you suppose was the number of the Orangemen who assembled upon that occasion?

Of actual Orangemen I should say there might be 12,000 or 15,000.

"Were they in uniform or armed?

I think I saw some persons in uniform. It was just after the formation of the yeomanry if I do not mistake. I was in the yeomanry uniform myself.

"Generally speaking, were the Orangemen who were reviewed by Generals Lake and Knox armed?

Generally speaking, they were, they could not be otherwise, because there was a great preponderance of the plain-coated men above the yeomanry; the yeomanry corps were small at the time and there was a mixed multitude of, I suppose, 20,000 persons.

"Do you mean that there were 20,000 other persons, independent of the 15,000 Orangemen, some of whom were dressed in scarlet?

Yes, a mixed multitude, cheering and taking a part."

Colonel Verner, M.P., who was examined on a previous day, gave a higher estimate of the number present. He said there were 30,000 Orangemen reviewed, and not less than 60,000 or 70,000 assembled on the occasion.

"They did not march as yeomen, but as Orangemen," and, he added, they received the thanks of General Knox.

"Were the thanks of General Knox given to bodies of troops composed of Orangemen or to the Orange Lodges in general, independent of the troops?

To the Orange body.

"To the whole society of Orangemen?

To the bodies of Orangemen.

"Were they given to men serving in arms for their country or to the institution of Orangemen?

I understood as Orangemen.

"It was to that body he returned thanks?

Yes, to the Orangemen.

"Thirty thousand men defiled before General Knox in their plain clothes as Orangemen?

Yes, as Orangemen.

The discrepancy as to numbers arises from the fact that Colonel Blacker spoke from personal knowledge, having seen the procession, while Colonel Verner repeated what he had heard not having been present. But the parade took place, with flags and music, and the Orangemen were thanked by General Knox. Although General (afterwards Lord) Lake was silent on this occasion, there is good reason to believe that he warmly approved of the forces he had reviewed; for subsequently, when requested, he allowed the Orangemen to hold their processions, not even objecting to soldiers taking part in them. He was too shrewd a military officer to look lightly upon a Reserve composed of brave and reliable men.

Another proof of the encouragement given by Government to the earlier Orangemen is afforded by the attitude and action of Dr. Atkinson, Grand Master of County Antrim. He was High Constable of Belfast, an "officer of the peace", and as much in the employment of Government as in that of the Grand Jury. Before the introduction of the Irish Constabulary, the High Constable and his subordinates were important factors in the Executive of every County, city, and town in Ireland. Their Executive duties ceased when the Head Constables, Constables, and men of the Irish Constabulary were appointed, and the force was organised. Dr. Atkinson was a High Constable, and in touch with the Government, and a more deserving officer Earl Camden and Lord Castlereagh could not have had. He enjoyed their confidence; they entrusted much to his wisdom; and assigned to him the control of many loyal enterprises. In the Correspondence(*) of James First Earl of Charlemont, the Grand Master of County Antrim, Orangemen occupied a prominent position. Of him the Rev. Edward Hudson, who had received permission to raise a corps of yeomen and become their Captain, writes to Lord Charlemont under date "1798, October 27, Portglenone" -

"I must mention to your lordship a strange circumstance which has come within my knowledge. Being in the house of a friend at some distance from this, a few days ago, I saw a paper

(*) *Historical Manuscript Commission 1894.*

empowering a person in that neighbourhood to keep arms, and signed: 'William Atkinson, captain commandant of the armed Orangemen of the County Antrim,' and directed: 'To all whom it may concern'. On inquiry, I found that Atkinson had asked the person to whom he sent that protection whether a company of 'Orangemen' and a proper captain could be had in his neighbourhood, adding t hat they should have arms. Atkinson is, I know, High Constable of Belfast, and 'Grand Master' of the County Antrim; but his title of 'captain commandant', and the phrase of 'armed Orangemen' puzzled me. I hear it said that this association has the direct protection of government."

In another communication. Mr. Hudson informs Lord Charlemont that "the Orange mania has broke loose amongst us, and spread with a rapidity almost incredible. It made its appearance here (but lately) through the means of a corps of yeomanry that has been quartered here some time.... within these forty - eight hours, the number of Orangemen is trebled in this town, I am confident. "Two of the Rev. Captain's own yeomanry appeared on parade with a little bit of orange ribbon in their hats; but, finding that the display was offensive to the captain, they did not repeat it. Yet, in the same communication Mr. Hudson informs Lord Charlemont that he believed the principles on which the Orange associations were formed to be those in which he had lived, and in which, by God's blessing, he would die.

Orangemen might not have been all that the Reverend Captain desired; but, it certainly was preferable to the seditious organisations that were willing to wound while afraid to strike. "That part of Derry which is next to me," he wrote to Lord Charlemont, "was for two days vibrating between rise and no rise, and was at last deterred by want of a leader, and by the failure of a partial rising near Maghera." In regard to Orangeism, Mr. Hudson seemed to be "vibrating" between joining and not joining, although he had evidence of the turbulence and crime promoted by the United Irishmen, murdering people in one place, burglariously entering houses in another, and spreading terror everywhere.

One of Captain Atkinson's exploits may be mentioned, showing the intimate relations of the Grand Master to the Government. Information had reached the Lord Lieutenant that, on a certain day in a certain house in Belfast, which was then a hotbed of treason, the Roman Catholics and Presbyterians having shaken hands as conspirators against England, there would be a meeting of delegates of the United Irish Society. Accordingly, instructions were forwarded to Colonel Barber, commanding in Belfast, and he went to the house, bringing with him a detachment of soldiers. Thither, also, went Mr. Fox, storekeeper of the ordinance, Lieutenant Ellison of the artillery, and Grand Master Atkinson.(*)

There were two committees sitting at the time in separate rooms, one of which was entered by Mr. Fox, and the other by Lieutenant Ellison, and papers were seized. In another room of the same house, Mr. Atkinson found papers belonging to a committee representing Donaghadee and its Vicinity. Some of the resolutions adopted by the United Men in that locality were of the most sanguinary character, and included the confiscation of the property of opponents, commanding farmers having "a redundancy of victualling" to bring it for sale at a price to be fixed by the Revolutionary Committee, and assuming power to appoint magistrates to act in concert with the Committee.

The whole programme of the Society was disclosed - its constitution, tests, mode of conducting meetings of baronial, County, provincial, and national committees, oaths, certificates, places of meeting and names of those who attended them, number of men enrolled, state of their equipment, amount in the war-chest. Later on papers were seized in Antrim and Down, and in one of them the current sign and passwords were given. The sign was, "the under button of the waistcoat to be taken out with the right hand, saying 'See'"; and the reply was, "Take out two under buttons with left hand, saying 'What'". The disclosures proved very useful to the Government, and broke the neck of the conspiracy; for, if Down and Antrim had risen simultaneously with counties in the other provinces it is hard to say what would have occurred.

Emergency Service to Crown as Orangemen in 1798

As we follow the course of history we shall see how admirably the Orangemen discharged their duty to the Government and to their own self imposed obligations. We shall see what they did, not as yeomen, but as Orangemen. Early in the year of the Rebellion, on the 25th of February,

(*) Report of Mr. Pelham's Secret Committee, 1797.

1798, a Loyal Address, in their behalf, was presented to Lord Camden, Lord Lieutenant of Ireland, assuring his Excellency of their fealty to King and Constitution. The words may be quoted -

"We, the loyal inhabitants of the province of Ulster, who have been styled Orangemen in remembrance of our glorious deliverer King William the Third, think it incumbent on us at this critical period to declare our faithful and steady attachment to his Majesty King George the Third, and to our valuable constitution in Church and State, as well as our gratitude for the blessings we enjoy under the present Government, and our happiness in the suppression of insurrection and rebellion, and the restoration of tranquility in this province. . We have no doubt of the sincerity of such declarations(*),and that the Catholics of Ireland, sensible of the benefits they enjoy, will not suffer themselves to be made the dupes of wicked and designing men for the most diabolical purposes, and we flatter ourselves that such declarations will be embraced, and have the happiest effects in other parts of this kingdom. Such conduct must be acceptable in the eyes of God and man. We declare most seriously that we are not enemies to any body of people on account of their religion, their faith, or mode of worship; we consider every peaceable and loyal subject our brother, and they shall have our aid and protection. Anxious to co-operate in preserving internal tranquility and repelling invasion should our foreign enemies be desperate enough to attempt it, we take this opportunity of declaring our readiness to undertake any duty in obedience to the commands of his Excellency the Lord Lieutenant.(**)"

The Address was signed by ten persons; William Atkinson, John Crossle, George Lendrum, Edward Butler, Anthony McReynolds, Samuel Johnstone, Richard Taylor, Hugh Watson, John Johnston, Abraham Dawson, William Hazleton, George Taylor, the ten signatures representing as many thousands of Orangemen. Lord Camden received the deputies graciously; thanked them for their pledge of fealty; and when the Rebellion

(*) *This refers to offers made by some Roman Catholics to assist in restoring tranquility if they were allowed to have arms, and were enrolled in bodies.*
(**) *Evidence of Lieutenant Colonel Verner M.P., 7th April 1835 to Select Committee on Orange Lodges, Mr Edward John Stanley in the chair.*

broke out on the 23rd of May following, his Excellency afforded the Orangemen an opportunity to undertake duty in obedience to his commands.

Belfast

Here is the statement published in the Belfast News Letter of June 15, 1798 -

"Since the insurrection broke out in this part of the country, upwards of 400 Orangemen have got arms, and been upon duty, under the command of Mr. William Atkinson, Grand Master for the County Antrim. It is but justice to remark that these men have conducted themselves with the utmost propriety and good conduct."

The compliment is good, although the diction is not the best; but the value of a gem does not depend upon the casket. At the date specified the paper was the property of a Scotch Company; and its announcement in regard to arming the Orangemen, and the tribute paid to their excellent conduct, are most valuable. The arming of the Orangemen was not for mere personal defence. It had much wider significance, and involved military duty. In the debate on Orange Lodges in the House of Commons, August 11, 1835, Sir William Verner, M.P. for County Armagh, read the following extracts from the Orderly Book of the Royal Artillery -

"Belfast, June 16th, 1798.
"Garrison Orders.
"Parole, Richardson.
"Countersign _____

"Detail for guard to-morrow, as usual.
"Field officer for the day, to-morrow, Lieutenant Colonel Kerr, Monaghan Militia.

"The Fifeshire will furnish 100 rank and file for guard to-morrow, the Monaghan 30, and the remainder by the Yeomen and Orangemen."

"Belfast, June 19th, 1798.
"The Belfast Yeomen are to do duty with the Fifeshire, which makes them upon an equal footing with the Monaghan Militia,

both corps having 500 men fit for duty. There are 228 Orangemen and Castlereagh Yeomen. One half of them are to be attached to the Monaghan and the other half to the Fifeshire."

The military status of the Belfast yeomanry is beyond dispute. They ranked in General Orders with the regular enlisted military forces of the Crown, and the Orangemen were of the same standing. Subjoined are extracts from the Orderly Book of the Belfast Cavalry, whose valour was displayed in the field. The corps was composed of the gentry and wealthy merchants of the town, who equipped and maintained themselves; and Belfast Orangemen acted with them or without them according to circumstances. The Orderly Book alluded to is in the possession of James Blakiston Houston, Esq., Vice-Lieutenant of the County of Down -

"G.O.(*)   Belfast, 11th June, 1798.
          "Parole, Stapleton.
          "Countersign_____

"Detail the guard to-morrow as usual. Field Officer for the day, to-morrow, Lieutenant Colonel Durham, Fifeshire Fencibles. Major General Nugent has appointed Captain Light, of the Fifeshire Fencibles, to be Commissary for the garrison of Belfast.
"The gentlemen of the Belfast Yeomanry Cavalry who serve without pay, are to receive rations for their horses the day they are on picquet. The ration is 14lbs of hay and 10lbs oats. The cavalry picquet is to be mounted entirely by the Yeomen Cavalry.
"The General Court Martial is adjourned until to-morrow at twelve o'clock.
"Twenty of the Orangemen to mount guard as last night.
"The York Fencibles and Newtownards and Comber Yeomanry, mounted and dismounted, are to do their proportion of duty to-morrow."

"G.O.   Belfast, June 14, 1798.
          "Parole, Victory.
          "Countersign_____
"Detail for guard to-morrow as usual. Field Officer for the day, to-morrow, Major Smith, 22nd Dragoons."

"G.O.   Belfast, June 16th, 1798.
          "Parole, Richardson
          "Countersign_____

*(*) Garrison Orders. (**Editor**)*

90

"Detail for guard to-morrow as usual. Field Officer for the day, to-morrow, Lieutenant Colonel Kerr, Monaghan Militia.
"The Fifeshire will furnish 100 rank and file for the guard to-morrow. The Monaghan 30, and the remainder by the Yeomen and Orangemen."

"G.O.   "Belfast, June 19th, 1798.

"The Belfast Yeomen are to do duty with the Fifeshire, which makes them upon an equal footing with Monaghan Militia, both corps having 500 men fit for duty. There are 228 Orangemen and Castlereagh Yeomen. One half of them are to be attached the Monaghan and the other half to the Fifeshire."(*)

These extracts will be interesting to the Orangemen of to-day. It may be noted that, in two cases the general orders in the Orderly Book of the Belfast Cavalry were copied word for word from the Orderly Book of the Artillery; and altogether the employment of the Orangemen, as Orangemen, cannot be doubted. They shared the perils, and helped to secure the object of the brief campaign. Their names were found in the lists of killed and wounded; they did all they were required to do in every other town and County in Ulster, and in other parts of Ireland, as well as in Belfast and County Antrim. In Portaferry, three Orangemen occupied, at a swivel-gun, the post of honour, which was to them the post of danger, the three having been killed in the performance of their duty. In Belfast, they were almost numerically equal to either the Monaghan or Fifeshire regiment; in courage they were not inferior.

One Orangeman on guard in Belfast was considered too vigilant. His post was at Ballymacarrett. Having heard the crash of a pane of glass, broken by accident, he immediately fired a shot, that being the signal of danger. Drums beat and trumpets sounded the alarm; Dragoons mounted and drew swords; infantry, yeomen, and Orangemen stood to arms; terror prevailed; for the Battle of Ballynahinch was at hand, and the cannons were shotted in High Street ready for action. The mystery was soon explained; the Orangeman was complimented for his zeal, but requested to be more cautious in future before rousing the garrison and terrifying the town. yet, in his General Order of June 20, General Lake thanked the army and yeomanry; but forgot the Orangemen.
(*) *Appears twice in the MSS. - (**Editor**)*

Co. Fermanagh

Let us now see what was done in Fermanagh, taking as our guide the records of Lisbellaw Orange Lodge, and forming therefrom an idea of what was done by the brethren in other parts of the County. The Lodge is No.315. The records of the year 1798 are in existence, and on the roll there are names of 196 members, who proved their loyalty, when "Erin's state was bad as bad could be." The first ten names on the roll are: Thomas Montgomery, of Sessiagh; William Farrel, Carry; Thomas Farrel, Carry; Thomas Trimble, Mullaghkippen; Ralph Shanley, Lisbellaw; John Dane, Killyhevlin [descendant of Provost Dane, who proclaimed William and Mary in Enniskillen in 1689.] After Mr. Dane's name is a note "Many have fled from the Orange cause." The list continues as follows:

Thomas Robinson, Ardess; Robert Strain, Edernyglash; John Farrel, Gola; Joseph Smith, Tattymacal; and so on till we reach the name of a member of a family always honourably identified with Orangeism - Hon. Arthur Cole, Florencecourt, the date of whose admission was 5th June, 1798. Next in succession on the roll came Daniel Kelly, Esq., Portora; Andrew Nixon, Esq., Silver Hill; James King, Esq., Corrard; Francis Dundas, Esq., Sub Sheriff; Lord Cole, Florencecourt, proposed by William Chartres, Esq., and initiated in the first degree 20th June, 1798. [His Lordship was grandfather of the late Earl of Enniskillen, Imperial Grand Master.] Continuing the list of names we have James Armstrong, Enniskillen; Captain Richard Maginnis, Chanterhill [Enniskillen]; Counsellor George Nixon, Nixon Hill; Gerard Irvine, Esq., Castle Irvine, [Necarn Castle, Irvinestown]; Captain Edward Archdale, Castle Archdale, [Lisnarick, Co. Fermanagh]; Lieutenant Henry Irvine, Lowtherstown, [Irvinestown].

The Purple List for 1798 contains 149 names; and it is worthy of note that, while Samuel Johnston is returned as Master, Mr. Robert Johnston, of Ballintaeson, was Chairman. From the records we learn that, on 10th April, 1798, a member was "excluded for ever," his offence being "improperly associating with United Irishmen, and keeping their Company." In the same year, on the 4th of December, a committee of twelve was constituted, to meet "in David Beatty's, on Monday ye 10th, 1798, in order to take into consideration a mode of Dress for this County".

The reference to the roll of membership shows the important position occupied by No. 315 in the County of Fermanagh. Among its members were men of high rank and title, representatives of ancient families, taking counsel with influential residents in town and country as to the best modes to maintain tranquility and check the spread of sedition. Of the 196 members, 149 had received the Purple, and representatively the whole County may be said to have been once a mouth in Mr. David Beatty's in Lisbellaw. The Lodge List for 1799 could show only 46 names, and 25 in the year 1800. This decline was not the result of lukewarmness in regard to Orangeism, but was due to the opening of new Lodges throughout the County, in more convenient localities. Noblemen and gentlemen, military officers, men of business, and farmers, could not be always expected to travel for miles to Lisbellaw when new Warrants could be taken out and Lodges formed at their own door. But before the "dispersion" No. 315 rendered useful service to the County and country at large.

The Fermanagh Orangemen were armed by Government as Orangemen, and the following is an example of the use they made of their authority. In one of the Lodge Books still extant, and at the head of a page, is a copy of a summons issued to the brethren -
"Notice.
"You and each of (you) are requested to attend at the lodge house of David Beatty, in Lisbellaw, by order of General Knox and Lord Corry - fail not at the order of your O.B. (*)
Given under my hand and seal."

Thus it appears that the Fermanagh Orangemen were amenable to the commands of Government, as the "order of General Knox" indicates. This statement is corroborated by other entries in the Lodge Book. One entry - September 7, 1798 - informs us that Sergeants Wade and Palmer complained that two Orangemen, whose names need not be repeated, "were called on to do duty as Orangemen (they having both arms and ammunition) as guard in the same manner as other Orangemen of this body acted during the Rebellion, and they having refused to do so, requested that they be tried by a committee." The request was granted; a committee of twelve was appointed; and the finding was that the accused were not worthy members. The verdict, dated 17th day of September, 1798, was signed by James Crawford, foreman, and Fellows. And this is not all. At the Lodge meeting on the 7th, arrangements were made to protect a large portion of Fermanagh, in a manner which attests the then military character of the Orange Institution, the Master acting as captain
(*) Orange Obligation. (Editor)

and appointing sergeants and corporals to carry out his orders in the several districts. Some of the entries may be quoted -

"James Chartres, of Corragh, is appointed first, and Alexander Montgomery, of Droles, Second Sergeant of the Lough-side Quarter, and John Fair Corporal.

"William Crawford and Edward Palmer are appointed first and Second Sergeants, and John Kennedy, Corporal, of the Kilmore side.

"William Rutledge sergeant of Maguiresbridge and its neighbourhood.

"Francis Johnston and Edward Wade Sergeants of Tanhouse Water and its neighbourhood, and James McCauley Corporal

(Signed)   "Samuel Johnston, Master."

The territory to be guarded was exposed to an invasion from Cavan, such an enterprise having occurred before; but the system adopted was complete, and afforded security to life and property. Similar arrangements were made all over the County, and the results were gratifying. Moreover, the services of the Fermanagh Orangemen were not confined to their own County. With Lord Cole at their head a large number of them acted as Volunteers in several engagements in the County of Wexford, and were present when the rebel camp on Vinegar Hill was captured.

Co. Cavan

At Vinegar Hill, too, was a strong body of Cavan Orangemen. Fortunately for County Wexford Orangeism had taken deep root in it when the Rebellion broke out. The Right Hon. John Maxwell Barry, M.P., who succeeded to the title of Lord Farnham, was at the head of the system, and worked it efficiently. In regard to County Cavan, the information was supplied by Mr. Charles Graham, in 1879. He was the oldest Orangeman in Cavan; was in his 91st year; and had been 74 years a member of the Orange Society. Born in 1788, he had a distinct recollection of the part the brethren had played before and after the Rebellion. Three of the yeomanry corps specially distinguished themselves. They were known as Ashfield, Cootehill, and Rathkenny yeomen. The first named was commanded by Captain James Moore Boyle, Tullynin House, and he was the oldest District Master in the County. All the officers of these corps were Orangemen - Captain Harry Clements, Higinbotham, Dawson, and Adams, the last three being members and officers of the Cootehill Orange Lodge; all the non-commissioned officers and men were Orangemen, with the exception of two privates in the Cootehill corps.

There were many Defenders and United Irishmen in the County; but they were careful to keep out of the reach of the Orange yeomen. Wherever the disaffected ventured to light a signal fire it was extinguished by the yeomanry and Orangemen. In this respect Ashfield was particularly famous; and the saying at the time was "there is a dark cloud over Ashfield", because no fires dare be lighted there.

On one occasion a man named Michael Donnelly fired a shot at a bonfire, and wounded a person named Moore, whose sobriquet was Blazer, and thenceforward the Orangemen of the locality were designated Ashfield Blazers. Soon after the establishment of the yeomanry force, the Orangemen, as Orangemen, formed themselves into separate bodies, each attached as Volunteers to a local company of yeomen, whose name was assumed. For this reason they were described as the Ashfield, Cootehill, Rathkenny, Belturbet, or Killeshandra Volunteers, the title being sometimes Loyal Volunteers, or Orange Volunteers, as the Captain of the yeomanry and the Master of the Orange Lodge might arrange. The Orange Volunteers were armed by the Government; and the several districts were patrolled by a specified number of Yeomen and Volunteers. In the Cavan Militia there was a large Orange element; and, in the earlier stages of the Rebellion, when the regiment was ordered to proceed to Dublin by "forced" marches, the Orange Yeomanry and Orange Volunteers promptly followed, and shared with the County corps the perils of many battles.

Co. Down

In the County of Down, which was a hotbed of disaffection at the time, the Orangemen rendered good service to Crown and Constitution. One example may be tendered, and the testimony is the more valuable as it was given by a gentleman who was not an Orangeman. The late Mr. James Dowsett Rose-Cleland, to whom reference has already been made, was a prominent Loyalist, and received repeated thanks from Government for his services; but his services. like those of other good men and true, were forgotten when men in high place began to worship at the shrine of Expediency, and he was deprived of the Commission of the Peace. Mr. Rose-Cleland commanded the Newtownards yeomanry at the Battle of

Saintfield, in the County of Down, and with his corps were the Orangemen of Newtownards. This is his testimony in a communication dated "Rathgael House, County Down, August 12, 1845"

> "Although I never was an Orangeman, they went with me to the Battle of Saintfield in the year 1798, and by their gallantry rescued the York Fencibles from utter destruction."

Co. Sligo

The York Fencibles was not the only regiment which the Orangemen rescued from grave peril. At the Battle of Collooney, in the County of Sligo, the career of French invaders and Irish rebels was checked by an Orange Lodge. When the French reached Tobercurry, after marching from Castlebar and Ballina, they were joined by their Irish allies, and the foreign invaders and domestic traitors made a stand at Collooney, or Coolaney. The records of their devastation included the plunder of the house of Mr. Perceval, one of the earliest initiated Orangemen of Sligo County. Early in the morning of the 4th of September, 1798, the peaceable inhabitants of the town were alarmed by the arrival of an army of fourteen hundred men, among whom were two hundred and fifty deserters from two militia regiments.

About eleven o'clock same day Colonel Vereker made his appearance at the head of about 376 men, with two curricle guns. The Colonel's force was composed of 220 of the Limerick City Regiment, 20 Essex Fencibles, 20 of the Loyal Sligo Infantry, 10 of the Ballimore Infantry, 16 of the Drumcliff Infantry, a troop of the 24th Light Dragoons, and detachments of yeomanry from the Tyrerill, Liney, and Drumcliff Corps. Co-operating with this small army were the master and members of Collooney Loyal Orange Lodge. All told, Colonel Vereker had under his command some four hundred men, regulars and irregulars, to fight fourteen hundred, two-thirds of whom were trained French soldiers, commanded by General Humbert, who had chosen his own ground and extended his line of battle to a place called Carrionagat, on the mountain adjoining, ordering them to · take shelter behind walls, ditches, etc. Colonel Vereker's strategy was excellent. The action began at 2.30, and lasted about an hour and twenty minutes. The fighting was desperate on both sides, and the loyal forces had to retreat. During the combat the bravery of the Orange Lodge was conspicuous; and at the critical moment its services were invaluable. An eye witness wrote in the Belfast News Letter of September, 1798 -

"Pressed in the above action by an army so much superior to ours, nothing could exceed the service rendered by Mr. Arch. Armstrong, who, at the head of twenty-two Orangemen, had taken so advantageous a position that the retreat of the cavalry was effectually secured."

At Saintfield the Orangemen protected the York Fencibles from being utterly destroyed, and at Collooney the Orangemen secured the retreat of the 24th Light Dragoons! The members of Collooney Lodge were thanked for their valuable service, and, on the recommendation of Colonel Vereker, the Master received a commission in the 71st regiment, rising by meritorious conduct to the position of a Field Officer. And this was not all. The French had suffered so severely - twenty-eight killed, and a large number wounded - that the grenadiers represented to Humbert the folly of continuing the struggle, especially as the Irish were deserting.

Co. Carlow

One additional example may be given of the services rendered by the Orangemen during the Rebellion. This time we pass on to the County of Carlow. On the 12th of June, 1798, the defence of Borris mainly devolved upon an Orange Lodge that had recently been formed in the locality. The master and members acted as auxiliaries to twenty of the Donegall Militia and one corps of yeomen. Borris House, adjoining the town, was made the head quarters of the small garrison, to whose successful gallantry an impartial historian has awarded well deserved encomium. The attack was made by a large body of insurgents from the camp at Lacken, and the town was set on fire in various parts; but the few troops and the Orangemen held the House, and the assailants were ultimately compelled to retreat.(*)

It would be impossible to estimate the value of the services rendered by the Orangemen in every province during the Rebellion. The sternness of their attitude and their unwavering loyalty had far reaching influence. Sir Richard Musgrave says -
> "When the French were at Collooney, and showed an intention of marching towards the metropolis, the Roman Catholics in the vicinity of Belturbet, in the County of Cavan, showed a disposition to rise, in order to join them; but as the Protestants of the

(*) *Memoirs of the Different Rebellions in Ireland.*

97

Established Church in that County are numerous, loyal, and well armed, and as they were mostly united in Orange Lodges, they would have cut the insurgents to pieces, had they risen there; they retired them to the Ballinamore mountains, about seven miles distant, and assembled there. Though the County of Cavan was in general very much disturbed by the Defenders, they, for the above reason, never dared to appear in the neighbourhood of Belturbet."

The Rest of Ulster

All the other counties of Ulster derived similar, perhaps greater, benefit from the presence of the Orange element. In this connection the testimony of Sir Richard Musgrave is most important. He says -

"The tranquility of the County of Armagh is chiefly to be imputed to the zeal and activity of the Orangemen. "The progress of the Antrim rebels was checked, and they were kept at the Antrim side of the Bann," all the bridges of that river having been well secured, and the boats drawn on shore to the Derry side by a party of Orangemen." In Donegall, the "united" Presbyterians and Roman Catholics were so much afraid of one another that they seldom went to bed at night, and finally numbers of the former "deserted their associates, joined the yeomanry, and became Orangemen". These are the words of the historian; but they are hard to reconcile to the Orangeman's oath. In the beginning of the year 1797, the loyal subjects of the County of Monaghan, "alarmed for their safety, began to form Orange clubs against the combination of traitors, who were constantly committing nocturnal robbery and assassinations". At first they were opposed by some of the gentry, who soon discovered their mistake, and threw in their lot with Orangeism. Then "the loyal subjects, animated by their united strength, struck the combined traitors with terror and dismay, and restored energy to the execution of the laws."

It was well for Ulster that, at a critical period in the history of Ireland, the Orange clubs were formed. In one place the Orangemen disarmed the Defenders; in another place they fought and conquered them; and in all places they stayed the progress of treason. East and South, as well as North and West, the lovers of law and order had good reason to be grateful to the

Orangemen. According to a Roman Catholic historian "fully two-thirds of the British force then enrolled were drawn from the gentry and the Orange lodges". Nearly every regiment serving in Ireland had its Orange Warrant; in one militia regiment of four companies there were four Orange Lodges, one to each company, while almost every yeomanry corps was an Orange Lodge in uniform.

Wicklow and Wexford

A remarkable illustration is afforded by Captain Gowan's yeomen, who were also Mr. Gowan's Orange Lodge No. 406, which had been organised a few months before the occurrence about to be referred to. In his description of a disaster that befell the Royal forces on their march to Carnew, in the County of Wicklow, June 30, 1798, the Rev. George Taylor says,

> "During this transaction, the Wingfield dismounted cavalry and infantry, under the command of Captain Hunter Gowan, came up with the rebels, and having no particular uniform, the enemy thought they were part of their own forces; but the yeomanry, seizing their opportunity, attacked them with great spirit, killed a number of them, and then retreated without the loss of a man."

This strange affair was explained by Mr. Robert Ogle Gowan,(*) who has stated that, on the occasion alluded to, Captain Gowan's yeomanry met in Lodge within his dilapidated mansion at Mount Nebo, and were initiating Lieutenant George Smith, of Cummer, when they were informed that about two hundred of the King's troops had passed on the road from Gorey, in the County of Wexford, to Carnew, to meet the rebels, who were reported to be advancing from Kilkelvin Hill. The Lodge was immediately closed, and the Master ordered his men to fall in. They were dressed in plain clothes, but they had brought with them their arms and a good supply of ball cartridge; and off they went, cavalry and infantry mingled promiscuously. On arriving at Ballellis - Colonel Puleston having meanwhile retreated with the remnant of his small army towards Carnew - the rebels were deceived by the costume, and cheered what they believed to be a reinforcement. Soon, however, the cheering subsided. The Wingfield men reserved their fire till they got within ten or twelve yards of the enemy,

*(*) Ogle R. Gowan, son of Captain Hunter Gowan, emigrated to Canada in 1829, becoming Grand Master of the Grand Orange Lodge of British North America. (**Editor**)*

99

and then they went to work with zeal and precision that, in a brief space of time, the rebels sought safety in flight. The victory must be placed to the credit of the Orange Society.

First Orange Lodge in Dublin

This year (1798) the Orange system had spread and taken root in most parts of Ireland. The encouragement given by Government was one cause of its growth; but the more important cause was its adaptability to the wants of the Protestants as a defensive organisation. Public instinct apprehended the outbreak of a rebellion which had been foiled in 1793, the arrangements of the disaffected not having been sufficiently matured, and in 1795 by the victory at the Diamond; but it was felt that restraint had lost its power to restrain the pent-up spirit of violence which was struggling to burst forth. Hence, the branches of the orange tree overspread Ireland. In the year 1797 the Orange system had more of less penetrated a large number of Irish counties.

During that year the first Orange Lodge was introduced into Dublin; the master was Mr. Thomas Verner, eldest son of Mr. James Verner, of Churchill, in the County of Armagh, and the secretary was Mr. Ryan, Captain of St. Sepulchre yeomanry corps, and author of the famous dinner-song entitled "The Protestant Boys", and beginning with:-"Tell me, my friend, why are we met here?"

Ryan was assistant to Town Major Sirr, a member of the Lodge, and was killed while capturing Lord Edward Fitzgerald in the house of a feather merchant in Thomas Street, Dublin, on the 19th of May, 1798. "Captain Ryan," says Sir Richard Musgrave, "received no less than fourteen wounds, of which he died a few days after, universally and deservedly lamented, as he was a man of great probity and firmness of mind, and a zealous loyalist."

The first Orange Lodge in Dublin could boast of having many worthy and distinguished citizens. Very soon a second Lodge was established, with Mr. John Claudius Beresford as master. Then other Lodges came in rapid succession. In the same year (1797) the Orange system had its representatives in Leinster, Munster, and Connaught, notwithstanding the terrible opposition it had to encounter. Wexford affords an example of the undying hatred to Protestants in general, and Orangemen in particular. Soon after the massacres, on the 20th of June, the following sentences

100

were carved on the rails of the portcullis of the bridge, the place where they had been perpetrated: "Sacred to the christian doctrine of sending orangemen to the meadows of ease, June 1798: The holy hereticks that were slain."

In Ulster, the system was invincible, and its popularity grew with its strength. One witness may be called, whose testimony is the more valuable as the author was prejudiced against Orangeism. Writing to Lord Charlemont, the Rev. Edward Hudson says "In Lisburn and its vicinity Orangemen are multiplying exceedingly, and in fact have an absolute dominion over their adversaries." From Glenavy to Lisburn the Orangemen were "completely triumphant, and increasing with astonishing rapidity". All the way to Ardee, in the County of Louth, he found the system "going on, but less in the County Down than elsewhere". In Jonesborough barrack, County of Armagh, there was a corps of yeomanry, a large portion of them Orangemen. The Ballymascanlan Volunteers, County of Louth, had been all United Irishmen; but their views were completely changed in favour of Orangeism. Finally, Mr. Hudson writes to Lord Charlemont, "In speaking of the astonishing increase of Orangeism, I forgot to mention the most wonderful part of it, that immense numbers of them are in Belfast." According to Mr. James Verner there were 1300 Lodges in 1796, so that in 1798 there would certainly be at least close upon 80,000 Orangemen in Ireland - all loyal, fighting men.

Organisation of Orangeism

It was well for Ireland that in such a critical period of her history she had so many thousands of loyal men, upon whom reliance could be placed. It was equally well for England; for if it had been possible for the Orangemen to have joined with the disaffected, no human being could have predicted the issue of the Rebellion. But the Orangemen could not do anything of the kind. Their love of Protestantism was too sincere, their fealty to Crown and Constitution too strong, to allow them to unite with traitors. In order, however, to make the Orange system more effective as a terror to evil doers, the common sentiment of the brethren aspired to have all the Clubs, or Societies, or whatever they might call themselves, whether Royalists or Loyalists, Boyne Men or Orange Men, welded in one grand confederation, whose affairs would be administered by a Grand Lodge to be kept in touch with County, district, and private lodges.

For this purpose a representative meeting was held in Portadown, a few miles from Loughgall, on 12th of July, 1796. The subject was earnestly discussed, and it was deemed advisable to allow the brethren time to consider the matter fully. Accordingly, the meeting was adjourned without arriving at any definite decision.

On the 12th of July, 1797, another general meeting was held in Portadown. A Grand Lodge was then formed, and the following were the first officers-

Captain William Blacker, Grand Master of Armagh;

Thomas Verner, Esq.,   Grand Master of Tyrone, Londonderry, and Fermanagh;

William Atkinson,   Grand Master of Antrim;

Thomas Seaver,   Grand Treasurer of Armagh;

David Verner,   Grand Secretary of Armagh;

John Crossle, Esq.,   Grand Secretary of Tyrone;

Mr. William Hart,   Grand Secretary of Antrim;

Mr. Wolsey Atkinson,   Acting Grand Secretary

The following resolutions were unanimously adopted -

1. That all Lodges shall pay an annual sum of three pence for each member, to defray the various expenses incurred by Mr. Atkinson in the issuing of Warrants.

2. That no Lodge shall be held without a Warrant, to be signed by Mr. Wolsey Atkinson, and a seal with the likeness of King William affixed thereto."

Subjoined is a fac-simile of the seal, taken from the original, cut in brass and is in the possession of the Wolsey Atkinson family. It will be seen that the seal bears the initials "W.A." (Wolsey Atkinson) and also the initials of his office "G.S.I." (Grand Secretary for Ireland).(*)

[Seal]

This was a step in advance. As a matter of right, Armagh had the honour of being the seat of Orange authority. In the County of the Diamond was formed the premier Grand Lodge; and the first Grand Master was Captain, afterwards Colonel, Blacker, of Carrick Blacker, the only gentleman of property at the Battle of the Diamond. But more was done on that memorable day. At the very time the Grand Officers were deliberating in Portadown, magnificent Orange processions were being held throughout Ulster. Twelve months before the Orangemen crept along byeways like children learning to walk. Now they presented a mighty front to sedition,

(*) The relic was lent to me by Mr. J. Buckley Atkinson, Solicitor, Portadown.

with heads erect, drums beating, banners flying. Twelve months had produced a great change in the relation between the Government and the Orange Society; and it was felt that the time had come for the Orangemen to make a display of their number and strength. Their action was stimulated by the approval of General Lake.

First Grand Master

Before giving examples of the processions, reference may be made to the worthy gentleman who filled the office of first Grand Master. Two sources of information are available; first his brief autobiography, and next an elaborate memoir published in a high class monthly periodical.(*)

From the autobiography (**) we learn that, a few days before the Battle of Antrim, young Mr. Blacker, then a student in Trinity College, doing duty with the College corps, was taken into the presence of the Secretary at the Castle, Colonel Stuart, afterwards Marquis of Londonderry, and was asked by him if he had not a certain degree of influence in his neighbourhood, as well as being a captain of yeomanry corps. The reply was affirmative, among the Orangemen in particular. The Secretary then inquired as to the number of persons he could bring forward in aid of the Government; and the answer was "one thousand men in a few hours".

Accordingly he was sent to the North by the mail coach that night with an order for 100 stand of arms, to be taken out of the depot at Charlemont, and a communication to General Knox. Immediately after arriving he placed the arms in the hands of the Orangemen residing near his own place. Subsequently, the arms were taken from the Orangemen, and placed in the hands of 100 men added to Mr. Blacker's yeomanry corps.

The result of the mission was getting together 12,000 or 15,000 Orangemen in Lurgan demesne. In the biography we are informed that the Blacker family traces its origin in Ireland to Blacar, a celebrated Danish chieftain. Mr. William Blacker, son of the Very Rev. Stewart Blacker Dean of Leighlin, was born in the old manor house of Carrickblacker, near Portadown, County Armagh. He was educated at Armagh Royal School, then presided over by Rev. Dr. Carpendale, "lamented Carpendale"(***), as his pupil described him.

(*) Dublin University Magazine 1841.
(**) Select Committee on Orange Lodges.
(***) Armagh, a Chronicle.

In 1797, Mr. Blacker proceeded from Armagh Royal School to Trinity College, through which he passed with good reputation. The biography, however, is wrong when he makes the First Grand Master one of the original members of the Orange Lodge formed on the field of the Diamond, as no Orange Lodge was formed for months after the Battle; but one thing may be stated without fear of contradiction; and that is, he was an earnest Orangeman, who never hesitated to avow his principles. Soon after taking his degree, Mr. Blacker obtained a commission in the 60th regiment, then serving in the West Indies; but, his health failing, he was compelled to return home. Then he received a company in the Armagh regiment. In 1806 he was promoted to majority; and in 1812 rose to the rank of Lieutenant Colonel.

In the latter end of 1816, he was appointed by his uncle, the late Sir George Hill, assistant vice-treasurer of Ireland. In 1826, at the death of his father - Dec. 1, aged 86 years - he came into possession of his ancestral estate, and discharged with zeal and ability the duties of a resident country gentleman, enjoying esteem of all creeds and classes. At the first issue of Warrants, in 1798, Captain Blacker received No.12.

He was born 1st September, 1777. He was High Sheriff of County Armagh in 1811; took an active interest in fiscal affairs as a member of the Grand Jury; was a J.P. and D.L. of the County; married, November 1810, Anna, eldest daughter of Sir Andrew Ferguson, Bart., M.P. He died in 1855; and there being no issue of the marriage, he was succeeded by his nephew Major Stewart Blacker, M.A., J.P., D.L., M.R.I.A., Barrister-at-Law, High Sheriff 1858-59, and for many years Secretary of the Grand Orange Lodge of Ireland. Now, we may supply examples of the processions.

Orange Demonstrations 1797

Belfast

The proceedings in Belfast were remarkable, and are taken from the report published in the local paper.(*) On Wednesday, 12th of July, 1797, a very great number of the inhabitants of Belfast and neighbourhood, denominating themselves Orangemen, assembled at an early hour of the morning to

(*) Belfast News Letter July 14, 1797.

commemorate the auspicious day. The different lodges moved from their respective places, and paraded through the streets with bands of music playing and colours flying, the more prominent devices on the latter being equestrian statues of the Prince of Orange, underneath which was the motto, "The glorious and immortal memory of William," the Crown and Harp surmounting the words; or the Crown alone, with the inscription "God save the King and Constitution". There were other symbols and other mottoes complimentary to Enniskillen, Londonderry, the Boyne and Aughrim.

Having marched through the streets in processional order, the lodges halted at the Linen Hall, thus forming an extended line of the artillery, Monaghan militia, and a numerous body of yeomanry, drawn up in Linen Hall Street, awaiting the arrival of General Lake, commander of the military forces in Ulster. When the General, with his staff, made his appearance, he was received in military style. The artillery stood to their guns; the militia and yeomanry presented arms, the band of the Monaghan regiment playing the National Anthem; and the Orangemen waved their banners, cheering lustily, assisted by crowds of spectators.

It was a mixed demonstration, composed of artillery, militia, yeomanry, and Orangemen - the forces of the Constitution arrayed to combat the forces of treason. The sight was novel, grand, and encouraging. From bugle and clarionet, from fife and drum, the gallant General heard for the first time Lilliburlero in its new title of "the Protestant Boys". Immediately after the parade the General and his staff took their seats in an open carriage to proceed to Lurgan, passing through Lisburn; but before he left the ground, a deputation of Orangemen waited upon him, and asked permission to complete their commemorative proceedings. The eminent soldier at once complied, reminding the deputies of the peculiar circumstances of the times, requesting them to conduct the ceremonial with decorum, and to maintain a peaceable demeanour.

He then started on his journey - properly a tour of inspection - escorted by the Belfast Cavalry to Lisburn, at which town the Lisburn Cavalry undertook escort duty to Lurgan. The procession in Belfast was resumed. In the van marched the artillery, followed by the Monaghan regiment, whose band played appropriate music; next walked the yeomanry, in whose ranks was some of the best blood of Belfast and surrounding district, and the rear was brought up by the Orangemen, some of whom wore orange sashes, some blue sashes, and some orange and blue combined.

The dress, the music, and the banners made the rear of the procession specially attractive. Ribbons and rosettes were profusely displayed, and many in the procession had aprons trimmed with the two favourite colours. Even the soldiers wore orange ribbons or rosettes, some adding orange lilies, which were generally fixed in the muzzles of the guns or bound to the tops of pikes or halberts.

It was estimated that there were between six thousand and seven thousand present, every one of whom exhibited an emblem of loyalty. Yet, this vast assemblage formed only a portion of the royal and loyal army, which was soon to risk all in defence of country, and, as the issue proved, to teach conspirators a salutary lesson.

The citizens of Belfast were proud to see the King's artillery and militia taking such a prominent part in the ceremonial, and their pride was increased when they observed their fellow townsmen - citizens - soldiers and Orangemen - file past, with stately step and manly bearing, the Linen Hall, the token of Ulster's industry and wealth, through Donegall Place, the town residence of the nobility and gentry of the North, and on through James's Street and Waring Street into Donegall Street, greeted heartily by the householders along the route, while the air resounded with the cheers of the multitude and cries of God save the King.

From almost every tongue the testimony was in praise of the demonstration. It inspired confidence; bade the peaceable to be of good courage, and the seditious to take warning; for the genius of Protestantism was aroused, clothed in orange and blue, able and willing to protect King and Constitution. The splendour of the demonstration was offensive to the enemy.(*)

(*) Dr Haliday, an accomplished man, who loved Ireland neither wisely nor well, caricatured the proceedings. In a communication to Lord Charlemont, dated Belfast "July 13 1797," he says the display was of Orange Boys Orange wenches and Orange children, "It was supposed that there might have been 3,000 of the motley crew including the various corps of yeomanry. I was exceedingly offended with the figures of the best of kings miserably depicted on divers banners, rather like a great fool."

Lisburn

When the General and his staff arrived at Lisburn, they witnessed tokens of another Orange display. This portion of the loyal army did not wait for the orders of the commander-in-chief. The Lodges were astir early in the morning marching hither and thither to welcome the brethren from the rural districts.

One who remembered the events of that 12th of July, and took part in the demonstration said that the greatest enthusiasm prevailed. Orange arches spanned the streets; Orange ribbons floated from hundreds of windows; young and old, male and female, wore Orange favours, uttered Orange sentiments, and chanted Orange melodies. When the procession proper was arrayed, the sight was grand. Among the Lodges present in full force were Nos.104, 121, 128, 136, 137, 138, 141, 152, 164, 170, 207, and 354, each exhibiting a banner, and stepping to the music of fife and drum.

The principal device on the flag was an equestrian statue of the Prince of Orange; the mottoes included King and Constitution, the glorious and Immortal Memory, Protestant Ascendancy, Enniskillen and Derry, Aughrim and the Boyne. As in Belfast, some of the Lisburn men wore orange sashes, some blue, and some orange and blue combined, while those who had not been initiated displayed orange ribbons, orange rosettes, or orange lilies.

The procession started before the General arrived, the rendezvous being the Maze, about three miles distant, cheered and encouraged as it passed along, many hundreds carrying arms at the shoulder. By the time the Maze was reached, nearly thirty thousand persons were present. All loyal hearts rejoiced at the magnificent turn out; for the safety of faith and home was secured, and the neck of rebellion was broken. No one any longer dreaded the United Irishman's password "Are you up?" The pageant was over by noon, and with abundance of sheepskin noises, to which we have become so well accustomed. There was no rioting. The music that broke upon the ear was ""Croppies Lie Down".

Lurgan

The General and his staff were more fortunate at Lurgan. there they saw what may be referred to as the grandest Orange display on record. It was chiefly organised by young Mr. William Blacker, at the request of the Government, after he had been to Dublin Castle, whence he returned home to rouse the County of Armagh. This demonstration has been already described. here it is sufficient to say that two general officers were on the ground - Lake and Knox - and they were delighted at the demonstration in Lurgan demesne. It was not displayed of military strength, but of orange strength. A few carried arms; another few wore uniform. Still, there were no military manoeuvres, no military parades, no military inspection.

All that occurred in this way was a march past, the commander-in-chief receiving the salute. The only emblems exhibited were Orange emblems; the only music heard was Orange music - God save the King, the Boyne Water, and the Protestant Boys. There were Orange Banners with the usual devices and mottoes; and the men who met in Sloan's after the Battle of the Diamond saw the grandeur of their organisation and the majesty of its principles.

There were many other demonstrations in Ulster; but the three named suit our purposes as they restored confidence to the Government and the community. "I have heard," said Mr. Stewart Blacker, "an aide-de-camp of General Knox, who was present at the meeting, and is residing in Dublin at this time [1835], General Owen, states that he went on that occasion from Belfast to Lurgan - that his impression of the state of the country was that it was in a most frightfully disturbed condition; that passwords, to which people would attach no particular or definite meaning, were prevalent among the peasantry, such as 'Are you up, are you up?' On their way from Belfast to Lurgan they saw several bodies of Orangemen in procession. In Lurgan Park, and in the presence of Mr. Brownlow, the proprietor of that domain, they received a body of nearly 20,000 Orangemen, who marched past before them; and on returning the next day to Belfast, a proper feeling of confidence seemed to be restored to the country; and instead of those indefinite words being used, the general expression that seemed to come from the peasantry was 'God save the King'." The day dawned on a spirit of distrust among the public; but the Orange demonstrations made a desirable change.

Statements of General Principles

In this year 1797, the Orangemen deemed it necessary to let the world know the fundamental principles of their organisation. Some leaders of the United Irishmen endeavoured to conciliate them, while others maligned them; and the reply was addressed to both sections of the enemy. At a meeting of Masters of Lodges, held in Armagh city, James Sloan presiding, the principles of the Society were stated in these terms -

"**1st.** We associate together to defend ourselves and our properties, to preserve the peace of the country, to support our King and Constitution, and to maintain the Protestant Ascendancy, for which our ancestors fought and conquered; in short, to uphold the present system and establishment at the risk of our lives, in opposition to the wicked schemes of rebels of all descriptions.

"**2nd.** Our Association being entirely composed of Protestants, has afforded an opportunity to people who undeservedly assume the appellation of Protestants, to insinuate to Roman Catholics of Ireland that we are sworn to extirpate and destroy them, which infamous charge we thus openly deny and disavow. Our obligation binds us to second and protect the existing laws of the land; and so long as we remain under the influence of that obligation, the loyal, well behaved men, may fear no injury of any sort from us.

"**3rd.** We earnestly request that the several Members of the Administration in this country will not suffer themselves to be prejudiced against us by the unfounded calumnies of unprincipled traitors, of ambitious dispositions and desperate circumstances, who detest us for no other cause than our unshaken loyalty; and who are using every exertion to increase their consequences and repair their shattered fortunes by plunging the kingdom into all the horrors of rebellion, anarchy, and civil war. And we likewise request the nation at large to believe our most solemn assurances that there is no body of men more strongly bound to support, or more firmly attached to the Government of the Empire, than the Orange Men of Ireland.

"**4th.** We further warmly invite gentlemen of property to reside in the country, in order that we may enrol ourselves as District Corps under them. And as two guineas (Government allowance) is not a sufficient sum for clothing a soldier, we entreat gentlemen to subscribe whatever they may think proper for that necessary purpose; many an honest fellow having no personal property to contend for, nor any other object but the laudable, patriotic ties of our Association.

"Abraham Davidson, Secretary"

The Master Orangemen of Armagh went still further. They appealed to the Government and to the nation in behalf of their loyal principles. In reply to an Address from the United Irishmen, they spoke plainly, and said -

Your plans and schemes are now before the Select Committee of the House of Lords and Commons, and such measures, we trust, will be adopted as will purge the land of your ringleaders. We are happy to find that lenient measures will be adopted towards those among you who, penitent for crimes ye have committed and the crimes ye intended to commit, throw themselves on the mercy of our rulers. The blood of four soldiers(*) of the Monaghan militia, who were shot a few days ago at Blaris Camp, and the blood of the unfortunate wretches who shall suffer for connecting themselves with you, will at an awful tribunal be demanded at your hands. In future we desire you will not call us friends, as ye have done in your last address. We shall not be your friends until you forsake your evil ways, and until we see some marks of contrition for your past conduct, neither do we wish to hold any intercourse with you, for 'evil communication corrupts good manners' as well as good morals. We are satisfied in the enjoyment of what we can earn by our honest industry, and neither envy those above us, nor desire to take from them a single farthing of their property. We wish you to be of the same mind.

(*) Their names were William McKenna, Owen McKenna, Peter McCarron, and Daniel McGillain. They had been tried by court martial and found guilty, and were sentenced to be shot at Blaris camp. The charge against them was "exciting, causing, and joining in a mutiny and sedition in said regiment;" and also for not giving information to the commanding officer (Colonel Leslie). The father of the McKennas had travelled from Truagh in the County of Monaghan, and being a tenant on the Colonel's estate, he was informed that his sons would be pardoned if they gave information in regard to the United Irish conspiracy in the regiment; but the old man refused, and the firing party did their duty. Musgrave says, Seventy of the regiment were corrupted in Belfast."

Similar principles were enunciated at a meeting of the Loyal Boyne Orange Association No. 315 held at Lisbellaw. Br. John Nall, Master, in the Chair. It was resolved

"That no person shall have admission into our Society until he shall give proper and satisfactory testimony as to his knowledge of any public or secret conspiracy against our Gracious Sovereign, King George the Third, his Illustrious House or the present Constitution as established by law, and that he is not a United Irishman, and never was sworn to the secrecy of any such Society, nor never will, unless at the hazard of his life; and that, if compelled, he will give information on sight of some magistrate or brother Orangeman, to the end that all dangerous and seditious persons may be brought to condign punishment.

"That we hold ourselves bound to our God and to each other, in no less a penalty than our Oaths, our Lives, and our Properties, to assist his Majesty King George the Third, and his lawful successors, against his and their enemies, whilst we reside in his Majesties dominions, and whilst he and they shall support and maintain the true Protestant religion, as declared and established at the glorious Revolution of 1688 to be the principle for the guide and government of all future monarchs of Great Britain and Ireland.

"That in case a foreign enemy shall invade this kingdom (as is now hourly expected) we subject ourselves, both by our unalterable principles and sacred oaths, to aid, assist, support, and defend his Majesty, our country, and religion, by all the means in our power, and at the hazard of our lives, if called upon by the civil, military, or other lawful authority.

"That, inasmuch as history and experience have truly informed us that the members of the Popish Church will keep no faith with us, whom they denominate "heretics"; and that they are also bound by the most sacred and religious ties to disclose and make known to their Priests at Confession, all secrets, whether of the State, or of ourselves; and also for the reason of their being almost universally disaffected to our good; that we do, therefore, declare that no member of the said Popish Church shall have any inheritance in our loyal brotherhood.

"That no member of this society shall screen or know of any "Defender" (so-called), "United Irishman", or "Deserter" from his Majesty's army or navy, without giving information thereof to some magistrate, or other person, that he may be given over to the laws of the land, or to the military authorities.

"That every member of this Association shall be at all times willing to receive arms from his Majesty's Government for the defence of the country, and to return them when required.

"That this Loyal Boyne Orange Lodge, No.315, will meet on the 1st day of July (Old Style) and 5th day of November in each year, provided we are so permitted by a Magistrate or the Commanding Officer of our County, in a full body, and decently dressed; and that we will march to whatever place of worship we may conclude upon, and return home peaceably and quietly, without molestation to the person or property of any person whomever - and we declare our reasons for so doing are in remembrance of King William the Third, Prince of Orange and Nassau, who restored to us our liberties and our properties, and who freed us from an arbitrary and cruel power; also in obedience to the wishes and example of our pious ancestors, which ordain the 5th day of November in every year to be kept as a day of Thanksgiving to Almighty God."

These resolutions expressed the sentiments of every member of the Orange Society. It cannot be said that they were unduly harsh towards the United Irishmen, as almost the like condemnation is to be found in documents issued by some of the parish priests and their people, who held meetings in various places in the North, and unsparingly denounced the disturbers of the peace.

An example is afforded by what occurred in the Roman Catholic chapel of Culfeightrin and Grange of Innispollan, County of Antrim, on Sunday, 3rd December, 1797. The Rev. Patrick Brerman, P.P., presided; and, in the paper issued, the parish priest and his flock said,

"Justly, regretting the disturbances which have outraged and disgraced the northern parts of this kingdom, and feeling sensible of the past errors which many of our body have been led into by the deep designs of wicked men styling themselves United Irishmen, who have been, and still are, the prime causers and sole movers of all the seditious proceedings which have torn and disturbed Ireland; and detesting and abhorring as we do from the bottom of our hearts both their seditious principles and diabolical practices, do hereby declare, and in the most solemn manner pledge ourselves to support with our lives and fortunes the blessed Constitution of this country and his Majesty's happy Government established amongst us, determined as we are to exert ourselves for the suppression of rebellion and sedition within our district."

The resolutions were endorsed by the parish priest and eight hundred Roman Catholics. A similar course was pursued by the Rev. Edward McMullan, P.P., and his flock in the parish of Rathlin. They, in addition to an expression of loyalty to the Constitution, avowed "sincere affection" for the Protestants.

The publication of such documents were grateful to the Orangemen of Lisburn and vicinity. Accordingly, they held a meeting on the 23rd of December, Br. John Johnston, of No.104 in the chair, and unanimously adopted a friendly reply in the following terms -

"We have seen with much satisfaction the Declaration of the Catholics of the Parish of Culfeightrin and Grange of Innispollan, in this County, of the 3rd of December, 1797, expressing sentiments which claim our earnest approbation and respect - loyalty to the King, and inviolable attachment to our excellent Constitution. Being the principles of our Association, we shall be happy to co-operate with loyal men of all religious persuasions in the zealous defence of these most invaluable blessings. Our conduct furnishes the best confutation of the gross calumnies which designing men, for obvious reasons, have industriously circulated against us. So far from harbouring religious animosity, we ardently wish to cultivate the good-will of our loyal Catholic fellow-subjects, and assure them of our sincere disposition to join our efforts with theirs, in resisting all hostile and traitorous attempts of foreign or domestic enemies to overturn our present happy Constitution."

This interchange of good feeling had a beneficial effect. It did not occur a moment too soon, as seditious affairs were assuming menacing aspects. There is no doubt it helped to thwart the schemes of the United Irishmen. The surrender of firearms had shown the dangers from which the North had escaped; for, in the course of a few months 129,583 weapons - guns, bayonets, swords, musket barrels, cannons, and pikes - had been seized or handed in voluntarily. No doubt the weapons were rude, and the military discipline of those destined to handle them was imperfect; but the disarming of nearly one hundred and thirty thousand men made the work of the Government easier than it would otherwise have been.

The arrangements of the disaffected had been so thoroughly disturbed that the rebellion, which was to have taken place in 1797, was postponed till a more convenient season. They received discouraging news from sea, the Dutch invading fleet having been defeated by Admiral Duncan. Still it was known that rebellion was merely deferred, not abandoned; and, with the concurrence of the French Directory, it was resolved to strike the blow in 1798.

Meanwhile, the Executive of the United Irish Society appointed a military committee, whose members were required to report the condition of Union regiments within their district; the number of miles from place to place; the roads, rivers, bridges, and fords; the military positions; the capacity of the towns and villages to accommodate troops; the movement of the King's forces; to announce the first appearance of the French, and immediately to collect their men etc. Loyal citizens generally were much alarmed, and many fled from the rural districts into the garrison towns. At this date there were twenty thousand yeomen and about thirteen thousand Orangemen in Ulster.

The Grand Lodge removed to Dublin

The activity of the disaffected influenced the minds of loyal men, who saw the storm approaching and determined to be ready when the cloud would burst. With this view it was resolved to remove the seat of Orange authority from Loughgall to Dublin, retaining to the village certain privileges on account of former services. On the 8th of March, 1798, a meeting of deputies from Orange Lodges and districts was held in Dublin. The following were present -
>   No.12, William Blacker, Grand Master, Armagh.
>   No154, Major Molesworth, Cavan Militia, County Master; Captain Moore, Cavan Militia, County Secretary.
>   No.176, Thomas Verner, Master, and Grand Master of Tyrone, Londonderry, and Fermanagh; Captain Beresford, Dublin Cavalry.
>   No.177, Quarter-Master Sergeant Hughes, Cavan Militia; Sergeant Hamilton, Sergeant Gibson, Master; Sergeant Gilchrist, same regiment.

No.222, Sergeant Little, Armagh Militia, Master; Sergeant MacClean, and Sergeant Holmes.

No.235, Sergeant Douglas, Armagh Militia, Master; Sergeant Sinclair, do.

No.413, Edward Ball, Master; J. Dojoncourt.

No.414, Lieutenant-Colonel Rochfort, Grand Master of County Carlow.

No.415, Sergeant-Major Gallogly, Fermanagh Militia, Master; Sergeant Prior, same regiment.

Thomas Verner, Esq., being called to the chair, the following resolutions were unanimously agreed to:-

Resolved - That it is highly advisable that a proper correspondence should be forthwith instituted between the different Orange Lodges in this kingdom.

Resolved - That it is advisable that a Grand Lodge should be formed for that purpose, to be held in Dublin.

Resolved - That this Lodge be called the Grand Lodge of Ireland, for correspondence and information.

Resolved - For the purpose of carrying the above resolution into effect, that each County should be divided into Districts by the Grand Master and the other Master of the County.

Resolved - That each District should have a District Master, to be chosen by the Masters of the Lodge in each district.

Resolved - That each County should have a Grand County Lodge, to be formed of the District Masters.

Resolved - That it is advisable that the Grand Lodge of Ireland should be formed by members, to be chosen by ballot by each County Grand Lodge, and that the Grand Masters of Counties, District Masters, and Masters of Lodges in Dublin, on account of their residence should be members, and that all Masters of County Lodges should be admitted as honorary members, and that each regiment, having one or more members, should have a power of choosing one member by ballot, to be a member of the said Grand Lodge.

Resolved - That the said Grand Lodge, when formed, should forthwith choose a Grand Master, to be called Grand Master of Ireland.

Resolved - That the Masters of Lodges, District Master, Grand Masters of Counties, the Grand Lodge of Ireland, and the Grand

Master of Ireland should be re-elected once in every year, one month previous to the first of July. (O.S.)

Resolved - That it is highly advisable that each Master of a Lodge should return the Number of his Lodge, together with the numbers that compose it, to the District Masters, to be returned by them to the Grand Master of the County, and to be laid by him before the Grand Lodge of Ireland.

Resolved - That it is advisable that the first meeting of the Grand Lodge of Ireland Should be on MONDAY, the 9th of April, 1798, to be held at the house of THOMAS VERNER, of Dawson Street, Esq., Grand Master of the Counties of Londonderry, Tyrone, and Fermanagh.

Resolved - That a copy of these Resolutions shall be sent to every Lodge in Ireland.

> Thomas Verner, Chairman, MasterLodge No. 176, and Grand Master of theCounties of Tyrone, Londonderry, and Fermanagh.

The removal of the Grand Lodge to Dublin was not intended to disparage the valuable services rendered to Orangeism by the Dyan and Loughgall. It was a purely strategic movement dictated by circumstances, the city being then the metropolis of an independent kingdom, the seat of legislative and executive power. Unfortunately, it was also a hotbed of conspiracy, which Orangeism was competent to check. Besides, the Orange system found favour with the nobility and gentry, who spent much of their time in their town residences.

A year had not elapsed since No.176 Lodge was brought to the city, the meetings being held at Harrington's in Grafton Street; and the membership included some of the most distinguished men in Ireland - noblemen, members of Parliament, clergymen, military officers, lawyers, and country gentlemen. On the roll were more than three hundred names, of whom the late Mr. Ogle R. Gowan supplied seventy six, apparently in the order of initiation. They deserve to be mentioned here -

> Thomas Verner, Esq., Master; Captain James Verner; David Verner, Esq.; John Verner, Esq.; William Verner (subsequently Lieutenant-Colonel Sir Wm. Verner, Bart., M.P.); Major Hamilton Archdall, Rev. Henry MacClean, John C. Beresford, Esq., M.P.; Rev. John Keating, Dean of St. Patrick's and Chaplain to the House of Commons(*); Richmond Allan, Esq.; Hamilton

(*)This refers to the Irish Parliment. (Editor)

116

Maxwell, Esq.; Alderman James Vance; Arthur Kelly, Esq., Sovereign of Armagh; Rev. Charles Cobb Beresford; E.A. Macnaghten, Esq., M.P.; Alderman Frederick Darley; Major William Bellingham Swan; Rev. John Leslie; Nathaniel Sneyd, Esq., M.P.; Sir John Ferns; Colonel J. Staunton Rochfort, Carlow; Henry Coddington, Esq.; Deputy Serjeant-at-Arms to the House of Commons; Henry Vaughan Brooke, Esq.; Henry Falkner, Esq., Carlow; Hon. B. O'Neill Stratford (afterwards Earl of Aldborough); Rev. Sir Henry Bruce, Bart; Alderman Jacob Poole; Rev. Thomas Knipo; Sir John Macnaghten, Bart.; Right Hon. the Earl of Annesley; John Stratford, Esq.; Earl of Athlone, admitted by acclamation, being the only remainder of the generals of King William; Rev. Henry Roper; Right Hon. Patrick Duigenan, LL.D.; Sir Jonah Barrington; Major Sandys; Wm. S. Hamilton, Esq.; Viscount Corry (succeeded as Earl of Belmore); John Henry Cottingham, Esq.; Rev. C. Palmer; Alderman Richard Mauders; Major Henry Charles Sirr; Hon. Captain de Ginkell (succeeded as Earl of Athlone); Gabriel Whistler, Esq.; Very Rev. Dean Blacker; John Giffard, Esq.; Hon. George Blaquiere; Rev. Henry Maxwell; Trevor Corry, Esq., Newry; Rev. William Lyster; Major Benjamin Woodward; James Corry, Esq., secretary to the Linen Board; Rev. Alex McClintock, Esq.; Serjeant-at-Arms to the House of Commons, Lieutenant Colonel Joseph Pratt; Sir James Galbraith, Bart.; George Ogle Moore, Esq.; Viscount Kingsborough (advanced to the dignity of Earl of Kingston); Captain Ryan; Alderman James; Rev. Mr. Brickle; Rolleston N. Cathcart, Esq.; Rev. Hans Caulfield; John de Courcey, Esq.; Rev. William Elliott; Rev. George Homan; Rev. Mervyn Pratt; Andrew Todd Patterson, Esq.; General Robert B. Sparrow; Henry Colcough, Esq., Carlow; Hon. Colonel Galbraith Lowry Cole (better known as General Sir Galbraith Lowry Cole); George Clibborne, Esq., Moate; Hon. Major Molesworth; Viscount Northland of Dungannon, County Tyrone; Hon. Thomas Knox, M.P. for Dungannon.

With such an array of names Orangeism attracted respect in Dublin, and success was secured to the Grand Lodge, whose first meeting was held at the residence of Thomas Verner, Esq., in Dawson Street, on the 9th of April, 1798. Mr. Verner presided; and the attendance included most of those already named. There were also present:

The Most Noble the Marquis of Drogheda; Captain Blacker, G.M. Armagh; Captain Hunter Gowan, G.M. Wexford; Right Hon. John Maxwell Barry, G.M. Cavan; Hon. J.W. Cole, G.M. Fermanagh, and M.P. for that County; Sir Richard Musgrave, Bart., G.M. Waterford; Captain Mervyn Archdall, M.P.; Edward Ball, Esq.; Samuel Montgomery, Esq.. G.M. of Kildare; Sergeant-Major Gallogly and Sergeants Price and Quinton, Fermanagh Militia; Sergeants MacClean, Holmes and Douglas, Armagh Militia; Sergeants Hamilton, Hughes, and Gibson, Cavan militia; and Wolsey Atkinson, Esq., Grand Secretary.

The chief business transacted was the appointment of Brother Samuel Montgomery and Harding Giffard to prepare Rules and Regulations for the use of all Orange Societies, thus setting aside the several County codes, and forming one code for the Orangemen of Ireland. The other matters disposed of had reference to the state of Ireland and the means to be employed to maintain the authority of the Government and the integrity of the Constitution. It was agreed to leave to Armagh certain privileges, guaranteeing that no Lodge could be held without a Warrant signed by Wolsey Atkinson, and bearing the seal of which a copy has been published. The meeting was then adjourned till November.

The 1798 Rebellion

Attack on Dublin

But before November came the storm burst forth. On the night of the 23rd of May the insurrection began according to arrangement. For days and nights previously the peasantry rudely armed had flocked into Dublin. The plan was artfully conceived. One party was to attack the camp of Lepaunstown,(*) seven miles to the south of the city; in an hour after, another party was to seize the artillery stationed at Chapelizod, two miles to the west of the city; an hour and a half later both parties were to unite and enter the city to co-operate with a third, and the Castle was to be surprised. Then the signal for the general rising was to have been given by the stoppage of the mail coaches on the northern, western, and southern roads.

It is said that Neilson, of Belfast, was to have commanded in the assault upon the Castle. The terrible calamity from which Dublin escaped may be
(*)Probably Leopardstown. (*Editor*)

imagined from the statements of Sir Richard Musgrave, who was there at the time, and, from a house in an elevated situation, had viewed through a telescope the fires on the Wicklow mountains, the meaning of which the disaffected could interpret -

"The sun never rose on such a scene of carnage and conflagration as the metropolis would have exhibited on the morning of the twenty-fourth of May; for it appears from various sources of information, presented to the publick by the secret committee of the house of commons, that the inhabitants of the counties of Dublin, Wicklow, and Kildare, were to have rushed into the city as soon as the insurgents had succeeded in getting possession of it, or as soon as the conflict had begun....All the loyalists would have been assassinated.... the accumulation of industry would have been pillaged; every monument of the elegant arts would have been defaced or destroyed; and whatever might have escaped the rapacious and destructive rage of the rebel plunderer, would probably have fallen a prey to the flames."

Fortunately, however, the Government had been informed of the plot, and adopted measures to avert the horrors it involved. Lord Edward Fitzgerald, brother to the Duke of Leinster, had been arrested in the house of a dealer in feathers in Thomas Street, by Mr. Swan, J.P., Town Major Sirr, and Captain Ryan - three Orangemen. His Lordship was then a wounded prisoner in the Castle. On the 19th, the day Lord Edward was captured, and on the 21st of the same month, the "Leinster Delegates" were seized in Bond's house in Bridge Street, which was followed by the capture of two leading conspirators, Henry and John Sheares, in the house of the former in Baggot Street, where also was found a Proclamation in John's handwriting, which was to have been issued on the morning of the 24th, complimenting the insurgents on their victory, and stimulating their worst passions.

Excitement was great in a proverbially excitable city; but it was soon allayed. Parliament voted confidence in Lord Camden's Administration; Lord Mayor Fleming acted on Lord Castlereagh's counsel; the troops of the line, the militia, the yeomanry, and volunteers were disposed of to the best advantage; the North did not rise at the signal; and the plot was shorn of its strength.

The Orangeman's services, which have been anticipated, were eminently successful in maintaining peace in Ulster. The Battles of Antrim, Saintfield, and Ballynahinch testify to the bravery of the Orangemen.

Co. Antrim

At Antrim, Lord O'Neill, a member of the Grand Orange Lodge, was piked on the bridge, and lingered for some days in Massareene Castle, where death put an end to his sufferings; Commodore Watson, a prominent Orangeman, narrowly escaped by his horse jumping over the bridge into the river; and it is not too much to say that the victory of the Loyalists was mainly due to the courage displayed by Mr. John Macartney, lieutenant of the Antrim yeomanry, and his brother Mr. Arthur Macartney, lieutenant of the Royal Irish artillery, sons of the Rev. Dr. Macartney, an Orangeman.

Their courage struck terror into the heart of Samuel Orr, who was in command of fifteen hundred rebels, and marched them back to Randalstown, to be heard of no more in Antrim. Samuel was brother to William Orr, who had been executed in Carrickfergus, and he was quite willing to wound the Government if opportunity were afforded; but the sound of the Macartney's cannon was enough for him and his men without coming into close quarters. When near the town the column halted, and the "Colonel" saw that the union of Protestants and Roman Catholics in the ranks was only apparent; for the latter demanded that the Orangemen in Antrim should be put to death, an act of cruelty to which the Protestants would not consent.

Defeated at Antrim, the rebels went to Ballymena and Donegore Hill. They were tired of war; surrendered their arms; and sued for pardon, which Colonel Clavering granted. The rebels in Randalstown marched to Toome; but nothing serious occurred there. From Ballymena an attack was made on Larne. There, however, the insurgents were repulsed by a detachment of the Tay Fencibles, aided by the yeomen and Orangemen.

Co. Down

Foiled in the County of Antrim, the rebels determined to show themselves in Down. The Battle of Saintfield, as it is called, was little more than a skirmish, although several of the loyal forces were killed. As usual, a false rumour was circulated that a rising had occurred where there was no rising, the object being to get the troops into trouble. Colonel Stapleton, at the head of a detachment of York Fencibles and some yeomen cavalry and infantry, with two pieces of cannon, marched towards the place indicated.

When within a quarter of a mile of Saintfield, passing through a hollow way, having high hedges on either side, the column was fiercely attacked by the main body of the rebels who were concealed behind the hedges and in adjoining plantations. The principle part of the column was allowed to go on unmolested; and then a heavy fire was opened on the rear, consisting of yeomen cavalry, who were thrown into confusion.

The Rev. Mr. Mortimer, vicar of Portaferry, his nephew, and seven or eight yeomen - Orangemen - were killed, as were Captain Chetwynd, Lieutenant Unit, and Ensign Sparks, while attempting to follow the Colonel and his grenadiers and cannon into the fields. After a short combat, the rebels fled to Newtownards, leaving 350 killed. There they became possessed of a quantity of baggage and ammunition; and, flushed with their victory over the guard, which was composed of invalids, they visited Bangor, committed depredations, took post on Scrabo hill, proceeded thence to Saintfield, plundered some houses, and halted in the town from the 8th till the 11th of June, when they marched to Ballynahinch.

During their stay in Saintfield, having a person named Jackson as leader, a party from the main body set fire to the house of Mr. Hugh McKee, about a mile from the town. The old man and his wife, seven sons, two daughters, a Roman Catholic man servant and a maid servant perished in the flames.(*) It was a Scullabogue in the North on a small scale; but, in cruelty, the deeds in Down and Wicklow were the same. It is alleged that McKee was an informer. The statement is untrue. He was a loyal yeoman; and his offence consisted in having prosecuted United Irishmen some time before. I knew his grand and great grand nephews, whose family tradition harmonises with the record now presented. Hugh McKee was not an informer; but a notorious informer led the murderers to his house, and witnessed the ghastly act of revenge.

The northern rebels made their final stand at Ballynahinch, then and now one of the most attractive small towns in Down. Henry Munro, having arranged so successfully the ambush at the defile near Saintfield, was elected generalissimo. He was a linen merchant of Lisburn, endowed with

(*) Twelve persons concerned in the tragedy were brought to trial before Lord Kilwarden, at Downpatrick Spring Assizes, 1799 and were found guilty. Three were executed on the Saturday following conviction; seven were left for execution on Saturday 6th of April; and two were respited until May. A cairn indicates the scene of the terrible occurrence.

excellent business capacity; but, as a military commander, his qualifications were inferior. There was, however, neither room nor time to choose. McCracken did not appear when needed at Antrim; Jackson had failed to turn Munroe's strategy to good account at Saintfield; and now the Lisburn linen draper was to have supreme authority. As adjutant to a company of Volunteers he had acquired some fame; but as a strategist in actual warfare he proved defective.

The rebels had two camps - one on the Windmill hill, about a quarter of a mile from the town, and the other at the house and in the demesne of Lord Moira. Their aggregate strength was estimated at 7,000, affording about 5,000 fighting men, of whom more than 2,000 were Roman Catholics. In both camps laxity of discipline and insubordination prevailed; and, as at Antrim, the apparent union of creeds did not produce unanimity. On the morning of the 12th of June General Nugent marched from Belfast with the Monaghan regiment, a detachment of the 22nd Dragoons, some yeomen infantry and cavalry, and a number of Orangemen as volunteers. Near Ballynahinch, Nugent's force was augmented by a portion of the Argyleshire Fencibles, another detachment of the 22nd Dragoons, and some yeomanry corps, under command of Lieutenant General Stewart, the latter proceeding from Downpatrick. Accompanying General Stewart were many Orangemen, one of whom was killed in combat.

The royal forces numbered more than 1,500 men. The first encounter took place at Creevy Rocks, about four miles from Ballynahinch, in the Saintfield direction, whither Munro had detached 500 men, commanded by a man named Johnson, the object being to check Nugent's progress; but they checked themselves, having been as thoroughly beaten that they dispersed, and never returned to Ballynahinch. The rebels had received their first defeat; still, they were not discouraged. The Windmill Hill was immediately vacated, and a portion of the royal troops took possession, and on the night of the 12th they set fire to the town, which was reduced to ashes. From first to last the combat was severe; but finally, victory perched on the standards of the Loyalists, in whose leading line were the Orangemen, as military men, yeomen, or volunteers.

It may be said of them, as Henry Grattan said of the Old Volunteers: "they were the saviours of the country." At Ballynahinch, the energy of disaffection in the North of Ireland was exhausted. The Presbyterians saw that there was no bond of union between them and the Roman Catholics,

2,000 of whom deserted the night before the battle; and it is alleged they remained about two miles off, on the Seaforde road, expressing satisfaction that the Protestants were destroying one another. A great many of the rebels, about 150, were killed; eventually Harry Munro and Henry Joy McCracken were executed, one in Lisburn, and the other in Belfast; and in the spirit of true wisdom, the people of Ulster set themselves to cultivate the arts of peace, having seen that the sickle was more profitable than the sword.

The South and West

The rebellion in the other three provinces was not so easily suppressed. In the North, the struggle, however reprehensible, was nominally for country; in the South the watchword was Creed, and Romish priests were the chief leaders. The services of the Orangemen may be inferred from the enmity displayed against the very name. Whenever a loyal Roman Catholic was found he was described as an Orange Papist. When Protestants were doomed to be murdered, they were first denominated Orangemen; or when, as in Killau, in King's County, a ruthless mob was collecting the Protestants, intending to burn them alive in the parish church, the proposed holocaust was styled an "orange pye". The Presbyterians of Ulster, as one of them stated on his way to the gallows, were too late in discovering the insincerity of their Roman Catholic allies.

The rebellion brought sorrow, in one form or another, to every Protestant household in three provinces, while thousands in Ulster suffered from its baneful effects. It has been estimated that 20,000 Loyalists were killed or banished from their homes, whose sites, in many cases, could no longer be identified. The loss of property was appalling, amounting in the aggregate to more than one million pounds, of which sum Antrim claimed £17,729-3-41/2; Down, £12,129-0-8; Londonderry, £7-19-3; Dublin, £25,829-16-01/2; Kildare, £97,090-2-11; Mayo, £120,523-11-41/2; Wexford, £515,191-8-5; Wicklow, £130,379-17. There were no claims sent by Armagh, Fermanagh, Monaghan, and Tyrone(*); but, with these exceptions, the Loyalists had suffered more or less in every County in Ireland.

(*) The peace of Armagh was maintained by the Orangemen. The rebels did not venture to rise in Fermanagh, because there were 6,000 Orangemen and other Protestants well armed. In Monaghan according to arrangement, the disaffected remained quiet, awaiting success in Longford which the defeat at Granard thwarted. Armed Protestants secured the tranquility of Tyrone.

Grand Lodge Resumes

The rebellion proved the necessity that existed for the Orange Society; and, therefore, the leaders resolved to make the organisation as complete as possible. With this view, the adjourned meeting was held in Dublin, on the 20th of November, 1798. Among those present were Thomas Verner, Grand Master; J.C. Beresford, Grand Secretary; R.G. Smith, jun., Deputy Secretary; H.A. Woodward; J.S. Rochfort, Grand Master of County Carlow; T.F. Knipe (Rev); Samuel Montgomery, Grand Master of Kildare; Harding Giffard; William Richardson; John Fisher; William Corbett; W.G. Galway; Francis Gregory. The names are given in the order in which they appear in the first authorised copy of the Rules and Regulations.(*)

In harmony with the resolution of the meeting on the 9th of April, Mr. Giffard and Mr. Montgomery had, during the interim, examined the codes local to Armagh and Antrim, in order to provide a general code for the Orangemen of all Ireland. The brethren named handed in their Report, in which provision was made for the working of the system. Here it is worthy of remark that, although circumstances led to many changes in the form of the Oath, and in the signs and passwords, the fundamental principles of the Society have remained intact.

The Society has spread throughout the British Empire; it is known in the United States of America and in other foreign countries; soldiers and sailors carry it to distant lands; and wherever it is known it is respected as a loyal, law-abiding organisation, whose doctrines may be compressed into five short words - "Worship God, Serve the King", or, as the double duty is expressed in the motto of the Enniskillen Family - *Deum Cola, Regem Serva.* The code from beginning to end is permeated by strong religious sentiment, and an ardent desire to support Crown and Constitution. No effort was made to conceal the thorough Protestant character of the Association. Religiously and politically, the Society stood on the lines laid down in the Act of Settlement; while the Oaths and Obligations were parallel to those imposed on the Sovereign.

There could not be much secrecy when the whole matter was placed in the hands of a printer, to be circulated among the brethren. The machinery was

(*) The original has a footnote reading "Appendix" but no Appendix has been found among the papers in the P.R.O. `(Editor)

124

exposed to public criticism; no effort was made to keep back anything except the signs and passwords, which were found necessary to distinguish friends from foes.

Forged Rules

The revised Rules and Regulations were so religious in spirit, and expressed such friendly feeling towards all loyal citizens, that the disaffected envied the popularity the Orange Society was likely to attain. Therefore, they set to work to blacken its character. Fabricated and false tests were represented as having been taken to exterminate Roman Catholics, and were industriously circulated throughout Leinster, Munster, and Connaught. The object was to excite the resentment of ignorant Roman Catholics; and it had the desired effect, as "the deluded peasantry were engaged the more rapidly in the treason."(*) Yea more, "every species of misrepresentation and sophistry was made use of to vilify the government, to extent the union, to shake the connection with Great Britain, to induce the people to look to French assistance, to exaggerate the force and number of the disaffected, and systematically to degrade the administration of justice in all its departments." Of the fabricated Rules and Regulations, the following is an example. The copy from which they are transcribed was found in the house of Marlay, a tailor in Hoey's-court, Dublin, and similar copies were frequently discovered on the persons and in the houses of United Irishmen. The document is appended to the Report of the Secret Committee -

> "**1st.** Resolved unanimously that each and every member be furnished   with a case of horse pistols and a sword, also that every member shall have twelve rounds of ball cartridges.
>
> "**2d.** Resolved, that every man shall be ready at a moment's warning.
>
> "**3d.** Resolved, that no member is to introduce a papist or presbyterian, quaker or methodist, or any persuasion but a protestant.
>
> "**4th.** Resolved that no man wear Irish manufacture, nor give employment to any papist.
>
> "**5th.** Resolved that every man shall be ready at a moment's warning to burn all the chapels and meeting houses in the city and County of Dublin.

(*) Report of Lord Castlereagh's Committee of Secrecy (1798)

"**6th.** Resolved, that any man that will give information of any house he suspects to be a United Irishman's will get the sum of £5., and his name kept private.

"**7th.** Resolved, that no member will introduce any man under the age of nineteen or over the age of forty six."

This is Marlayism, certainly not Orangeism. In the authorised copy of the Rules and Regulations not a word is said - and every word in the small volume is printed in the Appendix - about the exclusion of Presbyterians, Quakers, and Methodists. As a matter of fact, thousands of Presbyterians were and are, members of the Society.

The founders of the Orange Boys Society were all, or nearly all, Presbyterians, and they joined the Orange Men's Society after the Battle of the Diamond. Wilson, Master of Number One of the Dian, was a Presbyterian, and the members of the Presbyterian Church took well to the Institution. Many Methodists, at that time attendants at the services in the Established Church and the Presbyterian Church, were Orangemen. The Quakers were not excluded by any Rule of the Society. They excluded themselves. In later days, some of the most worthy Orangemen were members of the Society of Friends. There wicked design, however, succeeded in creating a deep rooted prejudice in the minds of Roman Catholics, high and low, against the Orange Society - a prejudice which the Orangemen have not been able to eradicate, no matter what they say or do. Although again and again refuted, the calumny has survived, and is the stock argument of those who labour to malign the Institution. Not many years ago, a bulky pamphlet was published(*) and in it were repeated some of the vilest calumnies against Orangeism. It was said, the Orange system "had existed previously as a secret society under the name of "The Peep of Day Boys". No statement could be more in conflict with fact.

The Peep of Day Boys were never really organised; the banditti accepted the services of all turbulent Presbyterians, and their depredations were felt by Protestants as well as by Defenders. The Orangemen never sympathised with them, and seldom allowed them admission to their Society. Mr. Healy did not stop at one calumny. He said "The original oath

(*) A Word for Ireland; by T.M. Healy M.P., Barrister-at-Law (Gill and Son, Dublin 1886)

taken by Orangemen was, 'In the awful presence of Almighty God, I, A.B., do solemnly swear that I will, to the utmost of my power, support the King and the present Government; and I do further swear that I will use my utmost exertions to exterminate all the Catholics of the Kingdom of Ireland'." Such an infamous oath was never taken by an Orangeman. On the contrary, the Orangemen bound themselves to protect all loyal subjects, irrespective of creed or faction.

Mr. Healy was not the first barrister-at-law who calumnated Orangeism. His attack is mild compared to that of Counsellor Sampson, an able man, whose talents were sadly misapplied. William Sampson, son of a Presbyterian minister,(*) was born in Londonderry in January, 1764. After completing his studies he settled in Belfast, became an United Irishman, contributed articles to the Northern Star and a serial called The Bee, and took a prominent part in professionally defending United Men when the law pounced upon them. He was arrested in 1798, and was among those to whom the clemency of the Crown was extended. From the Continent of Europe he removed to New York, where he practised as a lawyer, and died there at the age of 72. His literary performances included an effort to caricature Orangeism, whose secrets he professed to have discovered. His version is so ludicrous that a portion of it may be quoted -

"SECRETS OF THE ORANGEMEN"
Q. Where are you?
A. At the House of Bondage.
Q. Where are you going?
A. To the Promised Land.
Q. Stand fast yourself?
A. Through the Red Sea.
Q. What is your haste?
A. I am afraid.
Q. Don't be afraid, for the man who sought your life is dead.
Q. Will you hold it or have it?
A. I will hold it.

(*) Reid says he was the son of an Episcopal clergyman of Londonderry.

"SIGNS OF THE ORANGEMEN"

"Take your right hand and put it to your right hunch, turn round, saying, Great is the man that sent me. Then take your left hand and say, Welcome brother Prince of Orange."

A fouler slander never was published; and the best proof of the maliciousness and mendacity of the libel is derived from the fact that the author became ashamed of it. "The Memoirs of William Sampson," originally written in a series of letters to a friend, were issued to the American public in a confused condition. The first edition attracted such criticism that the second edition appeared in a somewhat improved form, omitting, among other rash statements, the parody on the Orange Society. A reprint from the second American edition was published in London in 1832, and the slander found no place in the small volume; so that the fury of the "Memoirs" destroyed itself at the first onslaught. It had no foundation in fact at any period in the history of Orangeism, as was demonstrated by the evidence of the Rev. Holt Waring, who laid bare the whole machinery of the system before the Select Committee of the House of Lords on the State of Ireland (1825). The wicked calumny, however, suited the object of William Sampson; and as he wrote it in "exile," no stronger testimony could be borne to the mercy of the Irish Government, in allowing an active agent of the treasonable United Irish Society to escape the fate which justly overtook less conspicuous offenders.

The Barristers-at-Law cannot be referred to as the only calumnators of the Orange Society. Historians of the stamp of Plowden and Madden did not permit Orangeism to escape. The former appeared to have thrown off all restraint when he touched the Orange question; and he paid for his reckless statements.

At Lifford Assises, 1813, a verdict was found against him for £5,000 in an action for libel brought by Mr. John Hart, who was grossly misrepresented in the History of Ireland. One action was enough for Francis Plowden, LL.D., who retired to France, glad to be released from the ghost of a Society, that he had slandered. Madden did his part in the slander line; but Plowden did more. Indeed, if the calumnies upon Orangeism were removed from his three volumes, one would contain all he had to say, and that one would be flat and stale reading. He dipped his pen in gall when about to write of the burnings and murders he attributed to Orangemen. It was fashionable in some circles to confine Orange outrages to Armagh;

but Plowden, inspired by Marlay's forged Rules, and Madden, deriving his information from a forged "Orange" oath(*), enlarged the scope of the incendiarism. Plowden says,

> "In the adjoining counties of Tyrone, Antrim, and Down the Catholics were hunted from their dwellings, their chapels razed or burnt, and their property was plundered or destroyed with impunity."

Nothing of the kind can be ascribed to Orangemen. Roman Catholic chapels and houses were wrecked in some places; but the Orangemen were not the wreckers. On the contrary, they were the first to condemn such outrages, and among the first to subscribe money to have the buildings repaired.

Take, for example, the County Antrim. The Hertford estate in that County was, and is, one of the best properties in Ireland, owned at the time by a loyal nobleman, occupied by a loyal tenantry, and administered according to the most generous interpretation of the "live and let live" principle. Plowden's opinion was that nothing good could be identified with the proprietor, the property, and the people, "It is to be lamented," he says, "that the Orange system was so zealously encouraged from the pulpit. The Rev. S. Cupples, of Lisburn, and Philip Johnson, of Derriaghy, were prominently zealous in evangelising the new code.

Deputations were sent from Armagh, to inoculate the new lodges with the new matter: and the eruption was exuberant." The North generally held out no hope to Plowden and his friends; for the Protestant gentry and people were united in self-defence. "Several persons," he alleges, " of great landed interest in those parts insisted upon their Protestant tenants and labourers becoming Yeomen and Orangemen. Such were the Marquis of Hertford, Marquis of Abercorn, Lord Northland, the Earl of

(*) Madden's Orange Oath is taken from a letter addressed by Mr. Fitzgerald to Mr. Church. The writer said, "I believe it to be the Armagh Oath. The Oath I do not recollect, nor did I at the time, understand it; it speaks of rivers of blood, of wading through the Red Sea, a brotherhood, etc." In other words, it was a jumble of the original initiatory ceremony which was abandoned.

Editor's Note: *The original initiatory ceremony taken over from the 'Orange Boys' was officially abandoned with the introduction of the New System in 1800.*

Londonderry, Mr. Cope, Messrs. Brownlow and Richardson, members for the County of Armagh, and other possessors of great landed estates in Ulster."

The statement is only true in part; but in this case Plowden would make the part equal to the whole. Many proprietors favoured Orangeism, and their reward was found in the peace that prevailed in their districts. Others did not favour the system: they nurtured the seditious adder, and it stung them. With respect to the destruction of private property, Plowden's ingenuity was suspiciously active and seriously false. One example may suffice. He mentions the case of two brothers named Brangan, Roman Catholics, tenants of Lord Hertford, whose houses, he says, were burnt, with their whole family of eight persons, and all their furniture, and he adds "the savage Orangemen encircled the flames to prevent escape." The foul libeller goes on, "Lord Hertford was then in Lisburn. Instant investigation and exemplary rigor were threatened. No punishment ensued." Why?

Because the perpetrator could not be discovered, and grave doubt existed as to the origin of the outrage, or whether it was not connected with some irregularity inside the house. The facts are: Thomas Brangan's, or Brankan's, house was burned, and in the house perished the two brothers and Anthony McCorry. A man named Joseph Burns was arrested, and at Carrickfergus Assizes, July 26, 1799, he was arraigned on a charge of having murdered John Brankan and set fire to the house; but after the fullest investigation he was acquitted! Instead of eight persons being burned, as Plowden states, there were only three; and there was no evidence to prove by whom the outrage was committed. It may have been the work of United Irishmen, or of Protestants, or of Catholics; more probably the guilty persons were void of all religion, disciples of Tom Paine, then popular among some classes; but it was not the work of Orangemen. The attempts made to identify one person failed, the affair was unsolved and closed.(*)

Dr. Cupples and Mr. Johnson

In this place a few words may be said about the Rev. Dr. Cupples and the Rev. Philip Johnson, whose lives were spent in works of piety and benevolence. Never were there in the Irish Church more exemplary clergymen. Both were members of the Orange Society; they associated with the brethren in public and private; preached sound doctrine to them

(*) Sentence completed by Editor

on anniversary days; and helped to evangelise the new code. Dr. Cupples fell in with Mr. Johnson's views, and on the 12th of July, 1799, preached to the brethren of Lisburn District. The title of the discourse is "The Principles of the Orange Association Stated and Vindicated"; the words of the text are, "Let not then your good be evil spoken of"; and here are a few sentences from the sermon -

"We should endeavour to accommodate ourselves, for the sake of peace, and as far as we innocently can, even to the prejudices of others....Though founded on the purest and best principles, and for the most patriotic purpose, the Orange Institution has been most undeservedly traduced and maligned, not only by its open and declared enemies, who are also the enemies of our happy Constitution in Church and State, but through their means by many loyal and well-meaning people, who are misinformed respecting its true nature and tendency, and whose good opinion we should be desirous of obtaining. It has been justly observed that the very best things may be misrepresented; and when once an outcry is raised against them, few people have either the candour to examine them impartially, or the courage to appear in their defence, on finding them injured in public opinion. They are afraid to patronise what is generally condemned, lest the singularity of their judgement should be misconstrued into an affection for the bad qualities imputed, however falsely, to the thing whose worth and utility they would otherwise assert'. . . . few things have suffered more unjustly from misrepresentation than the Orange Institution....If a steady opposition to French principles and Republican theories of government, which have deluged many nations of Europe with blood, be criminal, we plead guilty to the charge. If unshaken loyalty to our beloved and excellent Sovereign be a crime, we confess our guilt. If an inviolable attachment to the Protestant Religion, and a desire to secure the interest and prosperity of it by all fit and lawful means be reproachful to us, we certainly merit reproach. We reserve our present happy Constitution, and, disclaiming revolutionary projects, wish it to be perpetual.

We venerate the Protestant Religion, with Protestant liberality of sentiment towards those who differ from us, and disavow every species and degree of persecution. These, and these only, are the principles of Orangemen, and we are neither afraid nor ashamed to acknowledge them. They are not the visionary ephemeral

The Rev. Snowden Cupples M.A., D.D.
Rector of Lisburn 1796 - 1835. Vicar General of Down & Connor.

Rev. Philip Johnston, Vicar of Derriaghy, 1772-1833

productions of metaphysical subtlety; but have been long tried and approved by the sure tests of reason and experience. They are the old Whig principles, and held by us in common with every good Protestant in these islands. They were handed to us from our ancestors, and we hope to transmit them unperverted and unimpaired, as a precious inheritance, to our posterity. They have been the source of abundant prosperity and comfort to the land of our nativity for more than a century; and in the support of them we have   declared our readiness 'to shed the last drop of our blood'. We have no secrets to conceal, except the marks and tokens by which we know one another....To divulge these would destroy their utility, and therefore the knowledge of them is strictly and properly confined to ourselves.....I trust you scrupulously observe in all your meetings due order, sobriety, and decorum....Sense of duty and regard for the honour of your institution should make you careful to guide your steps with discretion, and conduct yourselves in all things as becomes those who have the interests of piety, religion, and civil order seriously at heart. By these means, and in these methods, we shall most effectually put to silence the ignorance of foolish or uninformed men, and extract the sting from the tongue of slander. We shall rescue our institution from the power of calumny to injure it, and render it truly and universally respected."

Such was Orange Dr. Cupples. He knew the Institution, and was competent to describe it. Every sentence in his sermon breathes the spirit of Christian sentiment. Dr. Plowden was silent in regard to the discourse, which was in circulation when the calumniator was at work; but it did not suit his purpose to refer to it, or to study the principles of an organisation he had resolved to misrepresent.

Rev. Philip Johnson

The attack upon the Rev. Philip Johnson was more virulent than that upon the Rev. Dr. Cupples. In addition to being Vicar of Derriaghy, he held the Commission of the Peace, which brought him into contact with turbulent persons. He took an active part in organising the Antrim Association; and when the Orange system appeared in the locality, he was among the first to join it. Moreover, he enjoyed the confidence of Lord Castlereagh, who visited Lisburn to consult with him; and, as we have seen, his loyalty exposed him to the bullet of the assassin.

Dr. Plowden says of him, "Besides encouraging his Orange parishioners in their orgies, the reverend gentleman attacked the house of Mr. James Cochran, a Scotch Presbyterian, a man of respectable character, and exemplary industry, at the unguarded hour of two o'clock in the morning, and hurried him to Carrickfergus gaol, where he languished twelve months, without even the remotest appearance of a crime, merely because he judged him a friend to the Catholics." Now, viler calumnies have never seen the light. The person referred to had given a good deal of annoyance in the locality, in which he was a stranger, and with the politics of whose people he had no sympathy. He proposed to send a delegate from the parish to what was called a representative assembly in Ballymena to make a new Constitution. In fact, he laboured to spread mischief in the locality three years at least before the "virus" was brought from Armagh; and Mr. Johnson remonstrated with him in vain.

Mr. Johnson was only expressing the wishes of his parishioners, who met at the parish church, on the 12th of January, 1793, Mr. Humphrey Clarke in the chair, and passed strong resolutions, avowing their attachment to the King, and pledging themselves "at the risk of everything dear to us, to be ready to support and defend his Royal Person, Crown, and Dignity, against all his enemies and opposers whatsoever." Yea more, they resolved - twelve out of five hundred persons dissenting - "that we consider it inexpedient and improper to send Delegates to represent this Parish at a County meeting to be held at Ballymena on Monday next." The resolutions had powerful effect in preserving Derriaghy, Lambeg, Lisburn, Magheragall, Ballinderry, Aghalee, Aghagallan, Maghremisk, Glenavy, Camlin, and Tullyrusk from the contagion of sedition and treason. When rebellion broke out there was no more loyal district than the parishes named.

The Rev. Philip Johnson was a magistrate as well as a clergyman, and warrants having been issued against a number of persons, one of whom was Mr. James Cochran, he was arrested and sent to gaol, Lord Castlereagh himself being in Lisburn at the time to see the orders of the Court of King's Bench carried out. Mr. Johnson, as a magistrate, was present at the arrest, and so was Lord Castlereagh. He had no choice in the matter, and there was nothing harsh about the proceedings. The slanders were based upon the reports of anonymous correspondents of the Press, a seditious newspaper published in Dublin, and whose editor was arrested at the same time as Priest Quigly, but contrived means to cheat justice. The Dublin newspaper was suppressed on the 6th of March, 1798; but its namesake in Philadelphia had nothing to fear, and continued the work of slandering the Orangemen, pouring its wrath especially on the Vicar of Derriaghy, whose blameless life did not save him from the attacks of the enemy at home and abroad. The pious soul of the Philadelphia Press was shocked to read resolutions passed in a meeting held on a Sunday in Derriaghy parish church. On the occasion referred to fourteen lodges were present, Mr. John Johnson, Master of No.164, presided; and the sole object of the assembly was to thank the Vicar for the sermon he had preached to them.

He was dear to them as a loyal clergyman, who had sympathised with Orangeism from the beginning, although at the time - Nov. 1797(*) - he was not a member of the Society,(**) but he had been Vicar of Derriaghy since 1772, and made it a rule to preach to the brethren in his own and neighbouring parishes on anniversary days. The esteem in which the Vicar was held may be inferred from the subjoined portion of the Address presented to him, signed by the chairman and Mr. John Morrow, grand secretary -

> "You, as a magistrate, boldly stept forward to stem the torrent, and as a minister of the Gospel took care to inculcate in your hearers that reverence for the laws of God, and respect for the laws of our country, that so much endear you to every lover of peace and good order. No wonder, then, that the malignity of United Irishmen should be directed against you - no wonder their black assassins should in the dark lift up their cowardly hands to deprive you of life, and the country of one of its best ornaments. Then it was, sir, that 'the Lord was your strength and your shield.'......We also may hope to be defended by that g r e a t and Almighty shield....We cannot, sir, conclude, as we address you as Orangemen, without assuring you, in the most solemn manner, that those base, scandalous, and wicked charges, so often thrown out against us, as being enemies of our Roman

*(*) In the original manuscript the year 1897 is given by mistake (**Editor**)*

(**) He was initiated in 1798, and soon after was elected Grand Chaplain. In 1803, he received the dignity of Grand Master of the County of Antrim, which office he held to the year 1810, when he resigned in favour of the Rev. Dr. Cupples, whose son the Rev. Edward Cupples, acted as assistant (or as the term now is Deputy) Grand Master.

136

Catholic fellow-subjects, are totally groundless. We appeal to them in whose neighbourhood we live - have we at any time injured them? no, the loyal and peaceable Roman Catholic will always find in us protectors. We will strictly adhere to our motto, 'Fear God; honour the King; and love your neighbour as yourself.'"

A portion of the Vicar's reply may also be quoted as an answer to this declaration of Orange principles and to Plowden's calumnies -
> "Gentlemen - The present awful and important crisis calls for the most strenuous exertions of every sincere friend to the religion, the liberty, and the well-being of his country. If I have in any degree contributed to avert the evils with which these invaluable objects are threatened - if by doing so I have exposed to danger, and suffered some personal injury from the desperate attempts of wicked men - I have in return received ample recompense from the consciousness of having endeavoured to do my duty - from that security in which, by the Providence of God, I hope our country is established; and from this very flattering testimony of your approbation. An invincible attachment to our most holy Religion, and to our excellent Constitution, settled under the auspices of our great deliverer, King William, unshaken loyalty to our most gracious Sovereign, sincere obedience to the laws, and universal benevolence to men of all religious persuasions: These, you solemnly avow to be the fundamental principles of your engagements as Orangemen. By persevering in a line of conduct consistent with these principles, you will do honour to your Institution; you will completely refute the calumnies with which your enemies have endeavoured to asperse your character; and you will take the most effectual means to promote the great end of your association - THE HAPPINESS OF OUR COUNTRY."

Another calumny circulated against the Vicar of Derriaghy may be noticed. It was stated by the Press and Mr. Plowden that he
> "went into the country at the head of an armed train, about November, 1796, and having discovered about twenty-four persons, men and women, busy in the God-like work of digging up the potatoes of a poor woman, immediately ordered them to desist, took a number of them prisoners, kept them in Lisburn blackhole, some of them even for three days, till they swore the oath of allegiance."

Here again truth is mangled for the purpose of blackening the character of a friend to the Orange Society. It is necessary, therefore, to meet fictions with stubborn facts. On the 6th of November, 1796, a Proclamation was issued in the hope of checking the progress of treason, which was promoted under various pretexts. It was announced in the State document that,

> "in prosecution of the said treasonable purposes, many large bodies of men have assembled, arrayed themselves, and marched in military order, and with military music, through several parts of said districts (County of Antrim included) under the pretence of saving corn, digging potatoes," &c. And Mayors, Sheriffs, Justices of the Peace, &c., were charged and commanded "to use their best endeavours to prevent, and where that cannot be done to discover and bring to justice those concerned in the aforesaid practices...and to disperse all treasonable, seditious, and unlawful assemblies."

The potato-digging scheme was specified in the Proclamation; and to Mr. Johnson, as a magistrate, the "command" of the Lord Lieutenant and Privy Council was communicated. At the date of the occurrence, he was under military protection, and had a small guard of Dragoons quartered in his house. Having received intimation that the benevolent potato-diggers were at work, he went, attended by a corporal and six Dragoons and a considerable number of the loyal inhabitants of his parish, summoned as a *posse comitatus*, to disperse the seditious gang, who had marched to the ground with military music, displaying a green flag.

These features of the enterprise were overlooked by the Press and Plowden. Moreover, the real facts of the case are misstated. Instead of "twenty-four persons" being engaged in the potato-digging, there were fifty or sixty; for Mr. Johnson and his party made prisoners of forty-four of the diggers, two or three of whom were released on making proper confession of their crime and promising not to repeat it. The remainder were detained for examination, and an express having been sent to the Marquis of Downshire, his Lordship assisted in the inquiry. The result was the discharge of eighteen of the offenders, all of whom, except a few young men who were excused, took the oath of allegiance. Twenty-six, who refused to take the oath, were detained till Monday for further examination.

On that day, Mr. Johnson having explained to them the nature of their offence, they expressed contrition, took the oath of allegiance, gave bail for future good behaviour and were released. The owner of the potatoes was not a "poor woman," but a man named Jeremy Galway, who had been charged with being a United Irishman, and had absconded to evade imprisonment, a constable having a warrant to arrest him. The alleged confinement in Lisburn blackhole is utterly untrue, as the prisoners were lodged in the Classical schoolroom, and detained only from Saturday morning till Monday evening, during which time they were supplied with fire and candle, and had plenty of bread and beer free of expense.

Burning R.C. Chapels

Concerning chapel burning on the Hertford estate in the County of Antrim, Messrs. Plowden and Madden wrote rashly and indignantly. No doubt, Roman Catholic chapels were burnt; but the Orangemen did not burn them. Mr. Plowden says the Rev. Philip Johnson encouraged "his Orange parishioners in their orgies." He encouraged them in good works; and in the unhappy crisis referred to he promoted a subscription to compensate the sufferers. The attitude of the Orangemen is displayed in their resolution and the action that followed its publication -

> "We, the subscribers, members of the Royal Boyne Society, called Orangemen, and others, friends of said Association, being informed that, since the commencement of the Rebellion, which has brought disgrace and desolation on many parts of the kingdom, the Roman Catholic chapels in the parishes of Derriaghy, Ballinderry, Glenavy, and Aughagallen have been set on fire, and nearly consumed, by some wicked person or persons unknown; and being convinced that said atrocious acts have been committed by the enemies of our king and country, with an intention of inciting the Roman Catholics of this neighbourhood to join in the Rebellion, or supporting the groundless calumny that Orangemen are combined to persecute their Roman Catholic brethren; whereas their great object is to preserve our excellent Constitution, and to promote the general tranquility and happiness of the country, having always solemnly avowed that they are enemies to none merely on account of Religious opinions. We, therefore, have contributed the Sums annexed to our names, towards repairing said Chapels, and we promise to pay double

the Sum of our present subscription for the discovery and conviction (within six calendar months from the date hereof) of any person or persons who have committed said crimes.

"Dated this 14th day of August, 1798."

The subscriptions amounted to £59 13s 10d, exclusive of what was contributed by the Marquis of Hertford, a warm sympathiser with Orangeism, and the list contained the names of such decided Orangemen as Rev. Philip Johnson, Mr. William Atkinson, Rev. Dr. Cupples, Mr. Henry Waring, Mr. Samuel Waring, Major John Watson, Mr. James Watson, Mr. Samuel Delacherois, and Mr. George Whitla. Out of the money received £13 13s were paid, November 25, 1799, to the Rev. John Devlin, for the Rock Chapel in Derriaghy; £13 13s, July 9, 1800, to the Rev. William Dawson, for the Chapel in Aghagallen; and £13 13s, August 30, 1802, to the Rev. William Crangle, for the Chapel in Glenavy.

The balance remained in Mr. Johnson's hands unclaimed till the year 1803, when it was disposed of according to the wish of the subscribers. In truth, so far from the Orangemen of that district entertaining ill-feeling towards their Roman Catholic neighbours, the very opposite was the case. Every name in the list was honourably connected with Orangeism and Protestantism in the North of Ireland.

All who knew the Vicar of Derriaghy were astounded at the slanders. He was advised to take an action at law against their author; but, being a minister of peace, he relied upon the testimony borne by a life spent in doing good to all classes in the parish. Urged by friends, the Vicar invited the Roman Catholic clergyman to become a witness, and the following is the evidence supplied -

"To the REV. PHILIP JOHNSON, Ballymacash.

"Reverend Sir,
    "In compliance with your wish, I made it my business, which I also considered to be my duty, to take the opinion of some of the oldest and most respectable of my hearers in the parish of Derriaghy, respecting the charge laid against you by Mr. Plowden.
    "Such as I applied to gave it as their unanimous opinion that said charges were unfounded, and that your conduct was entirely the

reverse; allowing that during a long period of time, upwards of forty years, you have acted as an impartial Friend, and an upright Magistrate, giving equal justice to all sects and denominations that appeared before you in that capacity, determining according to evidence, without favour or affection.

"The charge laid against you, respecting your conduct towards Mr. Cochran, they consider as malicious, and totally undeserving the smallest credit, being wholly a fabrication.

"Upon all occasions (when in company with the late Rev. Mr. O'Donnell), when the name of Mr. Johnson was mentioned, he paid you the highest compliments, allowing you to be a very proper, useful member of society, according to his knowledge of you, during the time of his having the honour of your acquaintance, which was not less than thirty years.

"You and the Protestants of your Parish, Derriaghy, in general, particularly during the unfortunate troubles which took place in this kingdom, showed themselves in the most friendly manner to the Catholics of the place, and rendered them every protection from time to time in their power, and always continued to live with them as good neighbours and friends.

"As to that part of the charge which unjustly says, that Presbyterians and others were outraged by Orangeism, for befriending the persecuted Catholics, such a charge they never heard of before.

"The Catholics justly admit they were guarded and protected at the instance of the Rev. Mr. Johnson, and his parishioners, and by a Yeomanry guard provided and paid by Government, which he had the goodness to apply for, by which means they were preserved in security and peace.

"The consequence has been, that the best understanding, mutual kindness, and benevolence, subsist between persons of all religious persuasions in the parish of Derriaghy.

"And to show, further, the good intention of the Rev. Mr. Johnson, to do essential service to the Roman Catholics, that he commenced and promoted a subscription, among the Orangemen and friends of that Institution, to assist in repairing the Roman Catholic Chapels, which had been burned during the Rebellion, of which subscription, Mr. Devlin, then parish Priest of said parish, received Twelve Guineas, to assist in repairing the Rock Chapel of Derriaghy.

"These assertions I think but a just tribute due to your merit, and to the rest of your hearers and be assured.

"Reverend Sir,
                    "I remain
                        "Your most obliged,
                            "And very humble servant,
                            "DENNIS MAGREEVY."
(Derriaghy, 7th of April, 1814)

Similar testimony was given by the Rev. Patrick Brennan, parish priest of
Culfeightrin and Grange of Innispollen, and by 900 of his people,
acknowledging the protection they received from the Cary Yeomanry; by
the Rev. Daniel McDonnell, P.P. of Ladye and Ardeclines, corroborated
by 900 of his congregation; and by other priests and people, who were
saved by the Orange Yeomanry from the vengeance of Defenders and
United Irishmen. Plowden's efforts to connect the Orangemen with the
wrecking of Roman Catholic chapels on the Hertford estate was more than
a failure. It recoiled upon the slanderer's head, and destroyed his reputation
as a historian.

Chapel Burning in Leinster

Precisely the same effect followed Mr. Madden's attempt to identify
members of the Orange Society as perpetrators of outrages of the kind in
Wexford, Wicklow, Kildare, Carlow, and Queen's County. According to
his estimate, thirty-five chapels were destroyed in the counties named,
twenty-two of them being in Wexford. He says the figures were carefully
copied from the original manuscript in the handwriting of Dr. Troy, R.C.
Archbishop of Dublin; but the number is alleged to have been too low; and
Mr. Madden appealed to Thomas Cloney's Personal Narrative of
Transactions in the County Wexford to show that thirty-three chapels
were burned in that County.

The number may be correct; but Cloney does not accuse the Orangemen
of having been the incendiaries. He distinctly states that the burning was
done "by the military and yeomanry in 1798, 1799, 1800, and 1801." In
addition, he says that a Protestant Church (Old Ross) was burned in
consequence of the murder of an unarmed Roman Catholic by the Ross
yeomen. Now, the facts are all against Mr. Madden. In the first place there
were no Orangemen in some of the districts affected, and in others very
few. If the conditions in the counties specified had been the same as those

of the Hertford estate the destruction of property would have been less severe. Reliable authority informs us that many Protestant churches were injured; and, as regards the dwellings of Protestants in the disturbed counties, few escaped the hands of the destroyers.

Sir Richard Musgrave supplies a list of thousands of Protestants murdered and their houses and property destroyed in County Wexford and elsewhere during the rebellion - clergymen, country gentlemen, government officials, artisans, and farmers. The country was wasted, and widows and orphans left desolate. The excesses of the military and yeomanry were provoked by the cruelty of those who had solemnly sworn to extirpate "the Protestant heretics." In relation to chapel burning, the case of Athy is suggestive.

That chapel was burned at a late hour one night in the month of August, 1798, but the deed was not done by Protestants or Orangemen. On the contrary, in Athy, as in Lisburn, the Protestant gentry, magistrates, yeomanry, and some of the townspeople offered large rewards for the discovery of the incendiaries. The offer was useless, and nothing transpired for a time; but eventually the truth was made known. Nearly two years after the occurrence, Timothy Sullivan, a private soldier of the South Cork Militia, volunteered for service in the regular army, and before leaving he divulged the secret. On the 9th of April, 1800, Sullivan was examined, after having made a communication to his sergeant, who informed Major Hennis and Captain Langton.

The deposition, sworn before a magistrate of the County Kildare, is summarised by Musgrave, who says the original is in the Crown Office; and that deposition discloses the facts. Sullivan was sentinel at the gate next a Mrs Dooley's house on the night Athy chapel was burned, and he was solicited by a person named James Noud to swear against three men - John McKeon, John Drill, and John Willock - a soldier of the South Cork Regiment, and two yeomen, as having burned the house. He refused, and was afterwards followed to Kildare by Patrick Kelly, a Roman Catholic priest, and Thomas Fitzgerald of Geraldine, who, having got him into a private place, offered him £400 to swear against the three persons named. In addition, they advised him to desert, and promised him protection. Again and again he was pressed to swear against the three men; but declined.

Subsequently, about the 14th of April, Patrick Dooley, James Noud, and James Hendrecan, all of Athy were committed to gaol. Dooley, according to the sworn deposition of another person, said he knew the cause of their committal, which was "that the said Dooley, with Mr. Kelly the priest, and James Noud, had offered Timothy Sullivan, a soldier of the South Cork Militia, £400 to swear against John Willock and John Drill, two of the yeomen, and a soldier of the South Cork, as Orangemen, for burning the chapel....and said Dooley further declared that he had mentioned the business of hanging said Orangemen to Thomas Fitzgerald of Geraldine, Esquire; and that said Fitzgerald replied, that if said three Orangemen could be hanged he would get him said Sullivan £400 from Government and make up as much more among themselves."

Drill and Willock were arrested; but no one appearing to accuse them, they were discharged, and immediately brought actions for defamation. After the chapel had been burned, stables were fitted up as a temporary place for the use of the Roman Catholics; but in three weeks the premises were burned. Then Captain Rawson, of the yeomanry corps, feeling for the distress of the Rev. Mr. Keegan, the parish priest, offered him the use of a large house he had recently purchased near the town. He accepted the offer, and the house was prepared as a temporary chapel; but no one would attend the ministrations of the priest in the house of a heretic.

The plot to hang the three Orangemen failed; Orangemen had no hand in burning the chapel, or the buildings fitted up as a temporary chapel; the burning was the work of Roman Catholics, to excite the worst passions of their co-religionists; and Musgrave says, "There is not a doubt but that many other chapels were burned wantonly in the night in the Province of Leinster, to throw the odium of it on the Protestants." Madden suppressed the truth, if he knew it; and if he did not know the truth he ought to have made inquiry before maligning a loyal body of men. His prejudices were stronger than his judgement, or warped his judgement; but the Orange Institution has survived the slanders which reflect discredit on his memory.

Presbyterian Loyalty

It would be unjust to the Presbyterians to quit the period of the Rebellion without making suitable reference to the help they rendered in suppressing anarchy and restoring order. Unfortunately for themselves and the reputation of their communion, many of the Body were among the disaffected; but, for the more part, they were of the Unitarian persuasion. The great majority of the laity of the Presbyterian Church were thoroughly loyal. They joined the yeomanry; presented addresses to Earl Camden, tendering his Excellency their support; expressed individually and congregationally their attachment to the House of Brunswick, and their fealty to Crown and Constitution.

The Ministers were like-minded; and prominent among them were Rev. Dr. Bruce, of Belfast, Rev. Dr. Black of Derry, Rev. Thomas Cuming of Armagh, Rev. John Thompson of Carnmoney, Rev. Joseph Little of Killileagh, Rev. R. Rentoul - worthy men, who delighted to walk in the footsteps of Kelso of Enniskillen. Those who took a different course were, as Dr. Reid has stated, "acting in opposition to the authority of the Church to which they belong."

All told, eleven ministers and probationers were more or less implicated in the County of Down, and seven in the County of Antrim; but of the eighteen only two suffered capital punishment. "The Covenanters," says Dr. Reid, "were quite as much involved. They had only eight or nine ministers in Ireland, and of these two or three were more or less compromised." For our purpose, however, the great fact is that the laity took well to the Orange Society; and to-day thousands of them are faithfully discharging their duties as Orangemen.

Here is a specimen of the lampoons circulated -
Black George from Comber, he is here
With prying look - with prying look,
He gormandises with the peer,
Oh, wonderous luck - oh, wonderous luck,
Bob Black of Derry beside,
Conceited doodle, conceited doodle.

Joe Little was a preacher bold,
He came from Killileagh;
For a month he his parish left
To pimp for Castlereagh.

First Organised Issue of Warrants

All the Orange Societies having been amalgamated in one Society under the government of the Grand Lodge of Ireland, the next step was to issue an uniform Warrant. A fac simile of an original Warrant(*) is given herewith; and it is, probably, the only one in the United Kingdom, or in any other part of the Orange world. It is certainly the only relic of the kind that I have seen, and is published as it was found in the Lodge Chest, after the lapse of many years, impaired by time, as the deformities indicate. No lapse of time, however, could deprive the document of its intrinsic value as a witness to the simplicity which marked the proceedings of the earlier Orangemen.

The typography supports the belief that we have here a copy of the Warrant issued by Mr. James Sloan of Loughgall, when the Society was struggling to get into existence. Mr. James Sloan and Mr. Wolsey Atkinson, of Portadown, were brothers-in-law. The seal, cut in brass, which the latter used officially as G.S.I. (Grand Secretary of Ireland,) is still in possession of the family, and through the kindness of Mr. J.B. Atkinson, solicitor, Portadown, I had the privilege of using it to restore to my original Warrant the stamp which was defaced to the right of the Royal Arms. A Renewal, bearing date "15th Day of September 1828," was issued to Mr. John Hyde, signed by "Ernest Grand Master; Enniskillen, Deputy Grand Master; Henry Maxwell, M.P., Grand Secretary; John Patterson, Deputy Grand Secretary; Henry Brooke, Grand Treasurer; Wm. R. Ward, Deputy Grand Treasurer." Instead of being printed on paper with ordinary types, the Renewal is a copperplate done on parchment, with an equestrian statue of King William in the place formerly occupied by the Royal Arms, and addressed to "Our well-beloved Brother Orange-Man, of the Purple Order, John Hyde." It was cancelled in March, 1850.

(*) I discovered it in a bundle of old papers placed at my disposal by Bro. George Jackson, District Master of Loughgall. His father bought the interest of the house owned by Mr. James Sloan, and in it he carried on a prosperous trade during a long and useful life. Among the documents were an Ernest Warrant, an original certificate, etc.
Editor's Note: *A copy of a fragment of one of these documents is among the papers in the P.R.O. It is headed by the Royal Arms and was issued to John Hyde, to hold Lodge No. 670 at Ballymagerny, Armagh, dated 3.9.1798 and signed by Wolsely Atkinson, Grand secretary of the Orange Society of Ireland.*

Among the symbols of the Orange Society, the Warrant occupies a very important position. It is indispensable in regard to the constitution and procedure of a Lodge, which may exist without a banner or a band; but no Lodge can be formed, and no business legitimate to the Society can be transacted in the absence of the Warrant, or a Dispensation pending the issue of the Warrant. Hence, before such a document quits the custody of the Grand Lodge, the strictest inquiry is made into the moral character of the applicant. Even after a brother has passed the scrutiny of the District and County Grand Lodges, and been installed as Master, the annual election of officers imposes serious restraint on all concerned. There is nothing that a Master prizes more than his Warrant.

The tilers at the head of a Lodge in procession, carrying drawn swords, which have been displaced by deacon poles, stepped out proudly; the fifer and drummer, whose music was alone heard in former days, were proud of their performances; the bannerman was proud; the chaplain was elated to display his Bible on a velvet cushion; but prouder than them all was the Master bearing his Warrant, the token of his superior office and undisputed authority. It may seem strange that a Number so late as 670 would be assigned to a man residing midway between the Diamond and Loughgall; but, in the beginning, the rush for these documents was very great. Diamond Dan was offended because he did not get No.1, and he had to wait for a long time, his turn not coming till No.600 was served out. At the first meeting in Sloan's, immediately after the Battle of the Diamond, no Orange Lodge was formed, and no Warrants were issued.(*)

In process of time, however, Warrants were issued from Loughgall; but Portadown soon assumed the ascendancy. The Bann and its historic Bridge were there; Mr. William Blacker was there; and there, too, were the manly fellows at whose head he marched to the Diamond. When claims for Warrants could not be satisfied, the applicants received slips of paper as guarantees that in due time the Warrants would be forthcoming. One of these slips was handed by Colonel Blacker to the Select Committee on Orange Lodges. The applications were treated on the principle "first come first served." As already stated, it was not an unusual thing for those who had travelled from remote parts of Ulster to have to remain in Loughgall or Portadown for days, sometimes weeks, before they received Warrants, even after having paid the price, which amounted to £1-2-9.

(*) See Page 25. (Editor)

There were from the outset Marching Warrants for the use of the army; and, owing to the ordeal through which the Society had to pass, and to other causes, new organisations were formed, each issuing its own Warrants, which led to the Duplicates and considerable trouble.

No.11

The history of some of the older Warrants is remarkable. For example, No.11, claimed by Armagh and Down is a history in itself. It is likely the original No.11 was issued by James Sloan in Loughgall, and was renewed in 1798; but the date "4th June, 1793" is clearly a mistake, as there was no Orange Lodge at the time. It was one year before Wilson began operations at the Dyan, and more than two years before the Battle of the Diamond.(*) Nevertheless, the Warrant has an attractive, illustrating what an earnest man will do to accomplish his purpose. Mr. Woods was born in Barnamaghery, County Down, 4th June, 1793, and was initiated in the Orange Association on 12th July, 1811, in Ballyalgin Lodge, then sitting under "dispensation" granted by Mr. Robert Browne, of Clough, District Master of Lecale. Mr Woods presided for many years over No.11, which was originally given, according to his statement, to the regiment then known as the 17th Light Dragoons, lying at Richill. The Orangemen of that regiment carried the Warrant with them wherever they went, and regularly held their meetings.

At Waterloo, the brethren of No.11, with one exception, fell fighting in the cause they were doubly sworn to defend. A few years after, the survivor was discharged on pension, and returned to Ireland. When he reached Lisburn, he made known the wonderful story of the Warrant which he had with him as the remainder of the Orange Lodge in the regiment, and the precious document was secured by James Bell, a brother Orangeman. Mr. Bell parted with it in favour of Mr. John Thompson, of Ballydian, by whom it was submitted to a County Down meeting, presided over by County Master, Mr. Crommelin, of Carrowdore. Its presence evoked the liveliest interest, and the brethren resolved that Mr. Crommelin should bring the document under the notice of the Grand Lodge of Ireland, soon to meet in Dublin, to ask their opinion in relation to its genuineness. After

(*) *It is now known, from a notice placed in the Belfast News Letter, that the Orange Club at the Dyan already had 138 members on 22nd. January 1793, with J. Wilson as Master. (**Editor**)*

careful inquiry, the Grand Lodge decided that the Warrant was genuine, and a renewal was granted to Mr. Crommelin for County Down, signed by Colonel Verner, Deputy Grand Master; William Stoker, Deputy Grand Treasurer; and Ogle Robert Gowan, Assistant Grand Secretary. The date on the Warrant is 24th August, 1824.

Immediately, Mr. Woods was satisfied as to the genuineness of the Warrant, he bought the right to it for Barnamaghery, obtaining a certificate of the transaction from Mr. Thomas Lloyd, of Downpatrick, County Grand Secretary. Mr. woods also secured from the County Grand Master authority to establish the Lodge at once, and it was installed on the 26th of October, 1826. Another renewal was signed by Ernest Duke of Cumberland, and another by the Earl of Enniskillen. All these are carefully preserved by the Lodge. The Barnamaghery Warrant was soon again in combat. When the Benevolent and Loyal Orange Institution was in being the Richill brethren produced their No.11 warrant and disputed the authenticity of the County Down No.11. But Mr. Woods defended his claim at an Orange meeting in Armagh, Mr. Taskard Keys, of Bloomfield, Donegal, presiding. A sub committee was nominated to examine the whole matter, and the right of Barnamaghery was established. Thenceforward, Barnamaghery men rejoiced in the possession of their Number, and the Lodge was presided over by Mr. Woods till his death. He was in many respects a remarkable man, esteemed by all classes, his Roman Catholic neighbours included.

On the 12 July, 1803, then a lad of 10 years, he was present with eight other juveniles at an Orange meeting at Edenavaddy, where 41 Lodges paraded under the presidency of Lord Charles Fitzgerald. Then and there he resolved to become an Orangeman and work for Orangeism, and he kept his word. He died on the 4th April, 1883, after having been for more than seventy years a worthy member of the Orange Society. His remains were interred with Orange honours. On the coffin were placed two Bibles and the flag of No.11 Lodge, and in the procession following the members of that Lodge were the members of 547 Ballynahinch; 550, Saintfield; 551, Clontinaglare; 568, Ballynaglave; 620, Spa Wells; 660, Glassdrummond; 703, Tullygirvin; 783, Moneyrea; 909, Carsonstown; 916, Mealough; 1207, Ballygowan; 1426, Carrickmannon; 1462, Barnamaghery; 1516, Leggygowan; 1545, Killinchy; 1607, Listooder; 1646, Ardmillan; 1661, Drumreagh; 1663, Ballymacreely; 1744, Ballykeigle; 1994, Moneyrea; 244, Comber; 567, Comber; 1035, Comber; 1036, Ballyknockin; 1037, Comber.

A great change had come over the entire district of country; for the green flag was hauled down and the Orange flag was in the ascendant. The office of Master, so long and faithfully filled by Mr. Andrew Woods, was assigned to a competent successor, Mr William Martin, whose connection with the Orange Society dates from the 13th of July, 1829, and who is in every respect qualified to discharge the important functions of a leader and guide of loyal men.

No. 859

The history of No.859 is quite as remarkable as that of No.11. It was originally issued as a Marching Warrant to an infantry regiment, whose services in the Crimea were conspicuous. Immediately after the terrible conflict at Sebastopol, Mr. Edward Rogers, Armagh, Grand Secretary, received by post a parcel containing an Orange Warrant and a letter from a native of Armagh, who had left the Royal Irish Constabulary and gone to the Crimea with the Army Ambulance Corps. The letter stated that the members of the Lodge met under the Warrant regularly at appointed times in a cave only known to themselves, and carried on their Orange business same as if they were at home. They paid their dues, initiated members, conferred degrees, and took counsel together on various matters.

The noise of the cannonade and conflicting elements overhead made the meetings more than usually impressive, and all the conditions were calculated to give a lasting impression to the form of initiation in the Purple degree. The Master of the Lodge always carried the Warrant about with him, so that the members, in the case of accident happening to him, or of his death, knew where to find the important document. This custom secured the Warrant, but not until it fell into the hands of some Turkish soldiers, who were near the Master of the Lodge when he fell mortally wounded. Immediately the brethren heard of the death of their Master they went to inquire after his remains. Seeing a number of Turkish soldiers together, gazing in wonder at a document with certain words on it which they could not read and an orange ribbon and a seal the meaning of which they could not understand, the brethren at once demanded and received the Warrant. Just then the person who had resigned the constabulary and joined the Ambulance Corps came to the spot, and being an Armagh Orangeman, he besought the brethren of the regiment, before Sebastopol, to send the relic to the home of Orangeism. Hence it was forwarded from the Crimea to the Armagh County Grand Secretary, who wrote its brief history, placed it in the Orange Hall of Armagh as a momento of the heroic Master, and a token of the strong attachment of the members to the principles and practices of the loyal organisation.

The Poleglass Forgery

But there is another side to the Warrants question. Sometimes they were unfairly treated by the enemy. A notable instance is in connection with what is known as the Poleglass Forgery; and, although the matter belongs to a later date, it may be dealt with in this place. There was nothing new in the statement that the Orangemen had taken an oath to exterminate the Roman Catholics. Such slander was a favourite weapon in the armoury of the disaffected, and was freely employed by them from the days of Marlay, the Dublin tailor.

The infamous obligation was known as the Extirpatory Oath; and frequently the calumny was revived. On the occasion to which reference is now made the revival was due to the inventive genius of a writer in the Belfast Monthly Magazine, a publication notoriously hostile to Orangeism. The mystery was revealed during the examination of the contents of a defunct pedlar's wallet; and the announcement occurred at the time that Orangeism, as we shall see, was the object of unscrupulous attacks in Parliament and through the medium of the press.

Being the very thing needed, the discovery was accepted as a strong confirmation of the base charges hurled against the Orange Society. At the beginning of the current century Poleglass was a village having some twelve houses, in one of which the members of L.O.L. No.170 held their monthly meetings. The village was about one mile from Dunmurry, and a quarter of a mile from Derriaghy Church in the County of Antrim. Among the earlier members of No.170 was Thomas Walker against whom, as an Orangeman, there was no cause to complain. He was connected with the staple trade of Ulster in a small way, travelling through the country selling remnants of linen. By profession a pedlar, the poor fellow jogged along from day to day, carrying his pack and vending his little stock to the best advantage, taking care to have in his possession a certificate of his membership of Poleglass Orange Lodge. In the beginning of the year 1811, Walker became ill in a house in the parish of Drumbo, near Lisburn, and his illness ended fatally - the pedlar died. After death, an Orange certificate was found in his wallet; and the enemies of Orangeism substituted for the genuine certificate a very clumsy forgery, which was published in the November number of the Belfast Monthly Magazine, 1813. The poor pedlar was a stranger and friendless; his wallet was ransacked; there was no one to testify to its contents; and to swell the chorus of slander against Orangeism a certificate was forged, and a besmeared seal was forged, the wicked object being to fasten an Extirapatory Oath to Orangeism. Subjoined are copies of the forgeries-

LOYAL ORANGE ASSOCIATION NO. 170

"We, the Master, Warden and Secretary of Loyal Orange Association No. 170, held at Poleglass, in the kingdom of Ireland, do certify that Thomas Walker did in June 1798, regularly receive the first, second, and third degrees of a true Orangeman; and that said Thomas Walker was in June 1809, duly served with notice to take the extirpatory oath; which he, the said Thomas Walker, in the presence of us, refused to take, although duly admonished thereunto. These are therefore to caution all Loyal Associations not to recognise him as brother under the present system.

Entered, 24th of June 1798   SEAL

Drew off, June 29th 1809

"Given under our hands, and seal of the Society, this 29th day of June 1809.

                    JOHN DUCKER   Master
                    JAS. REA   Secretary
                    WILLIAM MARTIN Warden

The writer in the magazine adds:-
        "At the foot there was a farther certificate, containing a general recommendation. He travelled with muslin for a livelihood, and his last words were, to be buried by Orangemen; but his request was not complied with. The certificate was said to be legible at the time of its being found. The original is now in our possession, but is so defaced, as is supposed by some drugs which were in a bottle found in the wallet as to generally illegible. Some attempts were made by chemical means to restore it, but without effect. unwilling to act the part of alarmists on any side, we hesitate to give full credit to the word extirpatory, having been used, at least, in the common acceptation. Yet we think the business require investigation, and that the parties whose names are mentioned as being signed to the certificate should explain the

business. We solicit farther information on the subject from anyone capable of giving it; and at present withhold a decided opinion. The certificate was some time ago laid before Sir Edward Littlehales, who recommended farther inquiries to be made quietly respecting the transaction".

Such was the wonderful disclosure of the Pedlar's wallet, designed to prove that Orangemen had sworn to extirpate the Roman Catholics of Ireland. The writer in the magazine hesitated to give full credit to the word "extirpatory", which might have read amatory if it had not been for the evil effects of the anti-Orange chemicals.(**a**) The calumniator himself doubted the genuineness of the word extirpatory; and he asked for inquiry into the case, which in the eyes of an enemy appeared so very suspicious. His fears were soon dissipated, and his anxiety relieved; for on the 10th of December, a few days after the liable was circulated, an unequivocal denial of the charge was published in the Belfast News Letter. After reciting the charge, the subscribers to the Certificate said -

"On any other occasion we should have passed over in silence and contempt anything issuing from the polluted sources of this malignant and self confuted publication; but at the present time, when every attempt is made to misrepresent and injure the loyal and patriotic association of which we are Members, we deem ourselves called upon thus publicly to come forward and to declare, that such a form of certificate NEVER existed among us, and that the words above quoted are a base, impudent, and audacious FABRICATION. We impeach the candour and honesty of those who would admit into their columns, on the mere "assertion" of anonymous authority, a paper exhibits on the face of it broad and glaring characters of absurdity and falsehood. The writer states, that "at the foot" (of the original) there was a farther certificate, containing a general recommendation of the said Thomas Walker, and, "that his last words were, to be buried by Orangemen".

Is it then to be believed, that the Society would have given a recommendation to their brethren of a man, whom on the same paper they had cautioned against recognising as a brother; or that the man himself would have accepted from the Society, and

(a) The chemicals vanished when a copy of the forged seal was left at the fine-art establishment of Messrs. Marcus Ward and Company, Belfast, by whom the fac-simile given in this Chapter was produced.

carried about with him, a paper cautioning his brethren against recognising him; or that he would, with his "last words", have requested to be buried by the members of a Society which had treated him so ill, and propose to him a test which he must have regarded with abhorrence?

"The real state of the case is this: a certificate (not a caution) was given by us to Thomas Walker, which ran in the usual form, viz: "That he had regularly received the degrees of a true Orangeman in our Association: that he conducted himself during his stay amongst us to the entire satisfaction of all our brethren; and that we, therefore, requested that all the regular Associations of the Universe do recognise him as such". This paper, it appears, after his decease, fell into the hands of "some respectable persons" in the parish of Drumbo, "who were sold on examining his wallet", but who seem not to have been friends to him, or to Orangemen as they refused to comply with his dying request.

At the time it was found that is in the year 1811, it is stated to have been injured "by some drugs which were in a bottle found in the wallet," and at that time, it "was said to be legible, but is now so defaced, as to be generally ILLEGIBLE." Under these circumstances, a pretended "exact copy" of it appears, not without a reluctant confession of the writer's conviction, or, at least, suspicion, of its want of "exactness", in as much as he states, that "some attempts were made by chemical means to restore the ORIGINAL, but without effect; which yet he has thought proper to publish, without once putting its authenticity to the test, by requiring the attestation, or giving the names of the "respectable persons" by whom it is said to have been taken. We have thought it a duty we owe, not only to ourselves, but to the Association to which we belong, thus to give a positive and direct confutation of this malignant calumny, lest, by getting abroad into the seditious papers, it might mislead the uninformed, the credulous, or the unwary. With the liberal and enlightened, the obligations, declarations, and object of our Institution, so often published to the world are amply sufficient to repel the horrid imputation here attempted to be fixed upon us; and which its enemies could not extract from it, even by chemical process. "The public will now judge of what material the "venerable and patriotic" print, in which this atrocious libel is inserted, is composed; and by what mean and infamous arts, a despicable and declining faction in this country would obtain their object.

JOHN TUCKER
JAMES REA
WILLIAM MARTIN

"Derriaghy, Dec. 6 1813".

Not content with this emphatic joint denial Mr. James Rea went before Mr. W. Hawkshaw, J.P. at Lisburn, on the 18th of January, 1814 and testified on oath, as the Secretary of Poleglass Orange Lodge No.170, that he had written the certificate, which was expressed in the usual form contained in the printed Book of Regulations viz., "That he, the said Thomas Walker had regularly received the degrees of a true Orangeman in our Association; that he had conducted himself during his stay among us to the entire satisfaction of all our brethren; and that we therefore, requested that all the regular Associations of the Universe do recognise and admit him as such".

The Secretary added -
"I also swear, that I never heard of an oath of extirpation being proposed in ANY Orange Lodge; and that such an Oath is contrary to the fundamental principles of the Orange Association."

To this solemn oath the following was appended:
"Sworn before me, one of his Majesty's Justices of the Peace for Antrim County.

"W. HAWKSHAW".
"Lisburn, 18th January 1814"

Mr. Healy's Attitude

Crushed at the moment it appeared, the vile calumny was revived and repeated from time to time. The latest example is afforded by Mr. T.M. Healy M.P. Barrister-at-Law,(*) who says "The Orange Order was

(*) A Word for Ireland. by T.M. Healy M.P. Barrister-at-Law. M.H. Gill and Son, 1886

founded in 1795, when George the Third recalled the popular Viceroy of conciliation, Lord Fitzwilliam.......It had existed previously as a secret society under the name of the Peep of Day Boys....... The original oath taken by the Orangemen was -

> "In the awful presence of Almighty God, I A.B. do solemnly swear that I will to the utmost of my power, support the King and present Government; and I do further swear that I will use my utmost exertions to exterminate all the Catholics of the kingdom of Ireland".

This is, to some extent, a new version of the Extirpatory Oath; and in his haste to get at it, Mr. Healy confused history. The brief Viceregal reign of Earl Fitzwilliam had nothing to do with the founding of Orangeism, except so far as inspiring false hopes, and stimulating the lawlessness of the Defenders and the United Irishmen. His Lordship arrived in Dublin, as the successor of the Earl of Westmoreland, on the 4th of January 1795 and he left Ireland on the 25th of March. He had barely time to show how ready he was to cut down "the upas tree of Protestant ascendancy" when he was recalled, and no Irish loyalist regretted his departure.

Mr. Plowden says Mr. Pitt "tantalised and taunted Ireland by the transit of Earl Fitzwilliam, and there is no doubt if his stay at the Castle had been prolonged a few weeks, the rebellion would not have been delayed till '98. It was to have been begun in 1793, but the plot was not sufficiently mature. Then it was fixed for 1795, and the Battle of the Diamond was really a test combat. Six months after Earl Fitzwilliam left Ireland the Defenders forced on the Battle and after it the victors sought security in union, which was named the Orange Society. The Peep of Day Boys were not Orangemen, and the Orange Society did not grow out of the Peep of Day Boys system. There was nothing agrarian about the faction, which was composed of reckless persons of the lowest class, who preferred plundering houses to honest labour. With respect to the Oath, it carries its own condemnation as a forgery. No Orangeman would have made use of the word "Catholics". He would have said Papists or Roman Catholics; and as the threat of sixty or seventy thousand Orangemen exterminating three millions of Roman Catholics, the whole thing is absurd.

Shortly after the fabricated oath had been circulated, an emphatic denial was published by the Earl of Enniskillen, Grand Master of the Orangemen

156

of Ireland and Imperial Grand Master. His Lordship addressed the following communication to the Times -

"Sir - My attention has been called to a pamphlet by Mr. Healey, entitled "A World for Ireland", in which, along with many other equally rabid and unfounded statements about the Orangemen of Ireland he states, in page 148, what he alleges to be the original oath of the Orange Institution, the closing words being "and I do further swear that I will use my utmost exertions to exterminate all the Catholics of the kingdom of Ireland."

"Now Sir I have been upwards of sixty years a member of the Orange Institution, and most of that time Grand Master, and I can and do declare that I never heard of the existence of any such oath. My father was Grand Master for several years before my election to that dignity, and I know that he was utterly incapable of belonging to an association bound by so atrocious an oath. I have communicated with members of the Society - the best informed on the workings and rules of Orangeism, and the oldest surviving members of this body - and none of them ever heard of the existence of such

an oath. Therefore, I firmly believe the statement to be utterly false - I am, sir, your obedient servant.

ENNISKILLEN I.G.M.
"Florence Court, Enniskillen, August 5 1886.

The late Earl of Enniskillen was a high minded nobleman and his testimony puts an end to the base calumny and atrocious oath. Originating with the Executive of the seditious United Irish Society, it never had and never could have, a place among the religio-political organisation and obligations of the Loyal Orange Institution. The Cole family is of ancient origin, dating back to a remote period in English, and still more remote in Continental history.

The first of the name settled in Ireland was Sir William Cole rendered eminent service to the State. He was a Captain in the Lord Mountjoy's army, and a gentleman of good repute, holding important offices in the government of Sir Arthur Chichester, who had an excellent opinion of his qualifications which was cordially endorsed by the Lord of the Council. In a communication to Sir Arthur, dated May 20, 1610, their Lordships state,

"They are satisfied of his [Captain Cole's] sufficiency to maintain a reasonable proportion, and are aware of his merits. And as he has a commission for the charge of His Majesty's boats in Lough Yearne (Lough Erne), and for the keeping of the Castle of Enniskillen, they suggest that he should be assigned a servitor's portion as near as may be to the said castle, which otherwise will be very destitute of demesne, as the lands neat adjacent to the castle have fallen to the lot of some Scottish gentlemen in the distribution of the precincts, and cannot be altered."

The Captain was not an ordinary adventurer. He bought the chief portion of his property; and immediately after the charter specifying the lands was issued he set about mapping out the town of Enniskillen, in the island of the same name. It is more than probable that Captain Cole took this step, in relation to forming the capital of Fermanagh, from a feeling higher than caprice, as there is presumptive evidence to support the idea that the place was of considerable importance in Pagan times, named after a Fomorian Queen, who was killed in open combat, not drowned as tradition alleges. But be this as it may, Cathlenn (Kehlen) wife of Balor of the Blows, was defeated in an attempt to dispossess the people, whoever they were, then in occupation of the island.

The Captain was knighted in 1617; was thrice sheriff of the County; represented it in Parliament; and his valour checked the progress of the terrible rebellion that broke out in the end of the year 1641. He raised and led the forces of Fermanagh, and his regiment is said to have killed 5,000 rebels in successive engagements. Before taking the field, Sir William narrowly escaped assassination. The story was written by Mr. Bothwell, house steward in Florence Court, at the dictation of the late Earl of Enniskillen, who had it from a descendant of one who was present on the occasion, and is worthy of being repeated, as showing that "God moves in a mysterious way His wonders to perform."(*)

(*) This is the remarkable story: "In the year 1641, Sir William and a great number of the Protestant gentry of the County Fermanagh, were invited to dine with Colonel Rory Maguire, who resided at Crevinish Castle in the barony of Lurg, in the said County. The castle was situated at the end of a straight avenue, the road being paved, and broad green plots on each side of it. As Sir William Cole dismounted from his horse, at the entrance, a man - I think named Coughlin - who was in some way previously

158

From the first appearance of the Family in Ireland, three centuries ago, till the present day, the members have been conspicuously identified with the maintenance of law and order. They took well to Orangeism, and laboured to promote its highest and best interests. The late Earl of Enniskillen was First Imperial Grand Master, Grand Master of Ireland, and Grand Master of County Fermanagh. His father was G.M. of Fermanagh, a Deputy Grand Master when the Duke of Cumberland was Grand Master, and, G.M. of Ireland. His son, the present Earl, is G.M. of Fermanagh; and his son-in-law, the Earl of Erne, is Imperial Grand Master, Grand Master of Ireland, Grand Master of Fermanagh, and a worthy Orangeman.

Orange Demonstrations in 1798

It is not too much to say that in 1798 Authority in Ireland trembled in the balance. In the County of Armagh rebellion was thwarted in 1795; but in 1798 the seditious spirit broke away from all restraint, and displayed itself in cruel aspects. But fortunately the Orange Society had become a mighty

---

connected with his family, took his horse, and, whilst doing so, whispered in his ear, "your horse will be ready in ten minutes." This, as you may suppose, in those times, was a sufficient warning for a man to be on his guard; Consequently, after the party sat down to dinner, Sir William rose to go out of the room. The host said to him, "I hope you are not going away, Sir William" or some such words as these. Sir William's answer was "I am obliged to retire for a short time; but you see I am not going, as I leave my hat and sword in the window". He went to the door where he found Coughlin with two horses saddled. They both mounted and galloped off, their escape not being discovered, as they rode on the green sward on the side of the avenue.

The remainder of the Protestant gentry, when they found that Sir William did not return, became alarmed, rose up in a body, and made their escape. They were too strong a party to interfere with. Sir William Cole and Coughlin rode direct to Enniskillen, where the latter gave a full account of the intended rising; Sir William sent it off immediately to the castle in Dublin, where it was the first intimation received on the subject. The plan of Maguire and the other rebels at Crevinish was, to fall upon the party after dinner when they had drunk plenty of wine, and massacre them all."
- Parliamentary Memoirs of Fermanagh by the Earl of Belmore.

power. In many places it was sufficiently strong to keep down disaffection; in all places it imposed wholesome restraint upon the turbulent. Sir Richard Musgrave says it "invigorated the arm of the civil magistrate, and completely checked the progress of treason."

General Knox "assured Government that the institution of the Orange Lodges was of infinite use, and he would rest the safety of the North on the fidelity of the Orangemen who were enrolled in the yeomanry corps." Colonel Blacker said, "I consider, in the first place, that the establishment of Orange Lodges was the first thing that checked the march of republicanism and rebellion in the North of Ireland when the United Irishmen were on foot; they afforded a rallying point for the loyalty of the country. I consider they have been productive of various advantages; besides, in a moral and religious point of view, I am sure that the discipline of these Lodges has gone far to prevent many young men from falling into vice of different kinds, such as intoxication. They had a character to support, and felt that they had a character to support. I am sure it brought many to read God's word, and to attend God's worship, who, but for that, would have been ignorant and idle."(*)

In relation to the period under consideration an eminent writer says, "The rough Orange Society saved Ireland once, in the end of the eighteenth century, and it must be called in to secure her safety in the end of the nineteenth. Let Lord Salisbury listen to the confession of Archbishop Trench, and be wise in time: 'I hate the Orangemen,....but I see in them the last hope of Ireland.' Let the preacher of cool, not to say cold, universal charity study the organisation of the unpolished Protestants whose 'illiberal fanaticism' he despises. He will find, like Mr. S. C. Hall, that in principle the Orange Society cannot be described as even uncharitable'."(**) One more testimony may be quoted. It is from the late Earl of Enniskillen: "At the time when it [the Orange Institution] was first framed, the north of Ireland was in a state of convulsion and disorder, and more afflicted with sanguinary and barbarous outrages than the worst parts of the southern districts were then or have been since. Under the influence of the Orange Society tranquility was restored, and security preserved, not to the advantage of Protestants only, but to the comfort and advantage of the

(*) *Evidence before Select Committee on Orange Lodges.*

(**) *The Radical Cure for Ireland (Blackwood and Sons 1890)*

Roman Catholic population also."(*) Of the Orangemen of 1798, Mr. Froude says, "They filled the ranks of the yeomanry, and, beyond all other influences the Orange organisation counteracted and thwarted the progress of the United Irishmen in Ulster, and, when the moment of danger arrived, had broken the right arm of insurrection."

The Orangemen, too, had something to say for themselves. In the earlier years of the Society they gave word for word, exposing slander to public condemnation, as base coins are nailed to a shop counter. The men of Dublin were the first to speak out. Their manifesto was signed by Thomas Verner, John Claudius Beresford, Thomas Bell, Isaac de Johncourt, and William James, Alderman. It repelled the malevolent falsehoods, and declared "in the presence of Almighty God that the idea of injuring anyone on account of his religious opinions never entered our hearts. We regard every loyal subject as our friend, be his religion what it may - we have no enmity but to the enemies of our country." The men of Newry followed suit; and most of the Counties and Districts did likewise. Yea more, they emphasised their words by magnificent public demonstrations, which struck terror into the hearts of the disaffected, who saw that those who had conquered at Antrim and Ballynahinch were not afraid to appear in public. Some advised the brethren to commemorate the anniversary of the Battle of the Boyne in their Lodge rooms; but they did not heed timid counsels. The demonstrations were large and enthusiastic.

Croppies Lie Down

Perhaps the most attractive, certainly the most unique display was at the Maze race course, convenient to Lisburn, the heart of the most English locality in Ireland. Thousands of the brethren from the populous and thriving towns in that part of County Antrim, and from convenient places in the adjoining counties of Down and Armagh, marched in full processional order, with banners unfurled and stepping to the music of fife and drum. The banners were the same as had been borne in the face of insurgents one month before; and the drums were, in many cases, those employed to beat the call to arms when danger was approaching. Now they were used in more peaceable service. A brother who was present on the occasion informed me of the enthusiasm that prevailed among all ranks. Firm in pace and lofty in mien, the brave men, some of whom had fought at Antrim

(*) *Grand Lodge Address, 1851*

161

and Ballynahinch, marched in good order, the fife and drum of each Lodge playing the new and popular air "Croppies Lie Down". The tune was heard at the Maze for the first time; and the words were accepted as an excellent reply to the United Irishmen's password "Are You Up?" As the Lodge filed past, ardent Orangemen added vocal to instrumental music, singing -

> "We soldiers of Erin, so proud of the name,
> We'll raise upon rebels and Frenchmen our fame;
> We'll fight to the last in the honest old cause,
> And guard our religion, our freedom and laws;
> We'll fight for our country, our King and his Crown,
> And make all the traitors and croppies lie down.(*)

The song had a wonderful effect in restoring confidence to the community. It was the very thing that was wanted to raise the drooping spirits of the Protestants living in isolated localities; for, taught by experience, they dreaded the return of turbulence.

The Orange Peer and Paddy

In September of this year(**) the Earl of Annesley was elected Grand Master of the County Down.(***) When the vote was conveyed to him, his Lordship expressed himself well pleased, and set to work immediately to spread the principles of Orangeism over his valuable estate. During one of his visits to the tenantry, a Roman Catholic had a call from the noble Lord, "Paddy," said the Grand Master of Down, "I am anxious to have all

*(*) The original has a footnote reading "See Appendix" but no Appendix has been found among the papers in the P.R.O.(**Editor**)*

*(**) This would appear to be 1798 (**Editor**)*

(***) Francis Charles, First Earl of Annesley, joined Lodge 176 in Dublin in 1797. The following year he founded Lodge 520 at Mount Panther, Clough, Co. Down, the family seat at that time, before they moved to Newcastle and later to Castlewellan. Lord Annesley served as the first Master of Lodge 520 and in 1798 became the first County Grand Master of Down. He held this position till 1803, when he was succeeded as County Grand Master, by Lord Lecale, Previously Lord Charles Fitzgerald. **(Editor)**

my tenants Orangemen. The Society is loyal, and its doctrines are sound religiously and politically." Paddy was rather surprised at the proposal, for he had been an United Irishman, and as such was present at the Battle.(*)

*(*) The rest of the text is lost but there is no doubt that the Battle of Ballynahinch is intended. (**Editor**)*

EDITOR'S APPENDIX

Among the Wallace Papers are several newspaper cuttings which have not been included in the above text as they refer to a later period. **Two** of them which refer to the year 1820 are included here, to preserve them for the future. The second newspaper cutting includes a note on the Cottingham Family. No indication is given as to the source of the newspapers.

1. "MEETING OF THE GRAND LODGE"

"In conformity with the intimation given by the Grand Secretary, the Grand Lodge met on 10th January 1820.(*)The Grand Officers at this date were:

Gen. Archdale, M.P., Grand Master; (**)
Alderman A.B. King, Deputy Grand Master;
Capt. Cottingham, Grand Treasurer;
Capt. Norton, Grand Secretary;
Capt. Fitzsimons, Deputy Grand Secretary;
William Stoker, Esq., Deputy Grand Treasurer;
Rev. John Graham, A.M., Grand Chaplain;

The matter in relation to the secrets having been considered, it was resolved that a change in the Orange system had become necessary, and the following were appointed a committee to carry the resolution into effect:- Alderman A.B. King, D.G.M.; Capt. Cottingham, G.T.; Capt. Norton, G.S.; Capt. Fitzsimons, D.G.S.; Lieutenant Colonel Blacker, G.M. Armagh; Joseph Greer, Esq., G.M. Tyrone; The Hon. R. Westenra,

*(*) This was a most important year for the Orange Institution. Most of the original members of Grand Lodge had died and a new leadership had emerged, which was determined to grasp difficult issues that had been left in abeyance for 20 years. A second "New System" was introduced with a new very basic and simplified initiation ritual for both Orange and Purple Orders. (**Editor**)*

*(**) General Archdale was the third Grand Master of Ireland having been elected in 1819. The second Grand Master of Ireland was the Rt. Hon. George Ogle M.P. who had succeeded Thomas Verner in 1801. (**Editor**)*

D.G.M. Monaghan; Capt. M.F. Johnson (Proxy) Antrim; Counsellor Fitzsimmons, M. 1638; Joseph Thetford, Esq., G.S. Monaghan; Robert Duncan, Esq., (proxy), Down; Lord Viscount Mountnorris, 1638.

The committee deliberated during three days, and the results were given in a thoughtful report and a valuable new addition of the Rules and Regulations."

2. "A NEW REIGN" (*)

"An address of loyalty from the Orangemen of England was published in the London Gazette of March 21st 1820, and presented to his Majesty who received it Graciously. The address adopted by the Grand Lodge of Ireland was presented by Major Cottingham Grand Treasurer was also graciously received by the King. This recognition of Orangeism by the Sovereign confirmed the brethren in England and Ireland in the high opinion they had formed of His Majesty. At the meeting of the Committee, on 17th June, the following resolution was carried unanimously:-

"That the thanks of the committee are due, and are hereby given to our worthy Grand Treasurer Capt. Edward Cottingham for his persevering attention to the interests and welfare of the Orange Order, and for his presentation of our Address to His Majesty on 7th June 1820, which Address has been received in the most gracious manner."

At the same meeting Addresses of Approbation were also voted to Col. Taylor, Grand Master of England and to Mr. W.A. Woodburne, Grand Secretary of England, who had been initiated into the New System, that he might communicate it to the brethren in that kingdom. On the application of Capt. Cottingham, a renewal of a Warrant under the New System was granted to Mr. E.L. Swift, who was authorised to act as Secretary to the Grand Lodge of Ireland within the realm of England. The Orangemen of Great Britain and Ireland were now united in one System; and the defeat of the treacherous intentions of improper persons attested the necessity

*(*) The longest reign of an English or British Sovereign, up to that time, had just ended after 59 years. On 29th January 1820 George III died and was succeeded by his eldest son, George IV. George III's 59 year reign has only been exceeded by Queen Victoria who reigned for 63 years. (**Editor**)*

and value of the Purple Order to maintain the purity of the Orange Society(*)

The Cottingham Family

Among the most zealous of the earlier Orangemen of Ireland were James Henry Cottingham Esq. Grand Treasurer of the supreme lodge, and Grand Master of the County Cavan, and his son Major Edward Cottingham, who succeeded to the office of Grand Treasurer. The family was originally seated at Cottingham, near Kingston-upon-Hull, Yorkshire, and mention is made of John Cottingham, of Yorkshire living in the year 1504. The Irish branch derives from James Cottingham, living in 1621. He left two sons, one of whom, George, was elected Fellow of Trinity College Dublin in 1627, and five years after was collated to the Prebend of Tehallon (now Tyholland) in the diocese of Clogher. He was rector of Monaghan in 1642, endured great suffering, and fled with his wife and four children to Dublin. He left four sons and two daughters. The second son, Capt. James Cottingham, served in the army in early life, and subsequently settled in Dublin, from which city he was forced to fly to Chester with his wife and four children in 1688. He presented to Christchurch Cathedral a silver verge, still in use."

(*) From 1820 onwards the Second New System abolished the ritual and the Degree of Purple Marksman, introducing the simplified or "Plain" Purple Degree. (Editor)